ROYAL
SHAKESPEARE
COMPANY

Sponsored by
ALLIED
DOMECQ

THE RSC/ALLIED DOMECQ YOUNG VIC SEASON

PENTECOST

DAVID EDGAR

**FIRST PERFORMED
AT THE OTHER PLACE,
STRATFORD-UPON-AVON,
12 OCTOBER 1994.**

This production is
financially supported by

And the whole earth was of one language, and of one speech . . . And they said, Go to, let us build us a city and a tower, whose top may reach unto heaven; and let us make us a name, lest we be scattered abroad upon the face of the whole earth.

And the Lord came down to see the city and the tower, which the children of men builded. And the Lord said, Behold, the people is one, and they have all one language; and this they begin to do: and now nothing will be restrained from them, which they have imagined to do. Go, let us go down, and there confound their language, that they may not understand one another's speech.

So the Lord scattered them abroad from thence upon the face of the earth.

Genesis, Chapter Eleven

The famous 72 languages into which the human race was split after the tower of Babel (at least by mediæval commentators on the Book of Genesis) each covered several nations or tribes, according to Anselm of Laon, pupil of the great Anselm of Canterbury. William of Alton, an English Dominican, speculating further along these lines in the mid-thirteenth century, distinguished among men between language groups (according to the idiom spoken), between generations (according to origin), between the inhabitants of particular territories, and between gentes who were defined by differences in customs and conversations. These classifications did not necessarily coincide, and were not to be confused with a populus or people, which was defined by the will to obey a common law.

E.J. Hobsbawm,
Nations and Nationalism since 1780

The (Bulgarian) government announced last week that, on an experimental basis, it would allow Turkish children to learn their own language as an optional subject.
The Guardian, 17 June 1992

A MESSAGE OF WELCOME FROM ALLIED DOMECQ

In our second year as principal sponsor of the RSC, Allied Domecq, the leading international drinks and retailing company, is delighted to be able to extend its support to allow the Company to bring a full season of work to London's Young Vic.

The RSC/Allied Domecq Young Vic Season will run in tandem with productions at the Barbican and Stratford, offering a varied programme from traditional to more contemporary works.

Allied Domecq's commitment from the outset has always been to work in close partnership to enable the RSC to become even more dynamic as a theatre company and to be able to offer its exemplary work to an even wider and more varied audience. This new and exciting initiative will allow Allied Domecq and the RSC to work closely together to fulfil these aims.

Our business is to provide enjoyment and we certainly hope this will be reflected by the performances. We also hope you will be encouraged, as a result, to join us again at future productions.

Michael Jackaman, Chairman of Allied Domecq

We are delighted to welcome the RSC back to the Young Vic. It is appropriate that a company often in the vanguard of world theatre should present its work in one of Britain's most intimate and dramatic theatre spaces. Past RSC productions that have electrified our unique auditorium include *Macbeth*, *Measure for Measure* and *Othello*. The start of this RSC/Allied Domecq Young Vic Season is marked by the world premiere of *Pentecost* by David Edgar, which has been acclaimed as one of the most serious and brilliant plays in recent memory and as 'the best play of the year' by the *Independent* and the *Independent on Sunday*. It is a fitting and exciting start to this excellent season. What makes the RSC's visit so special is that it brings together a great company and a great theatre for a whole season of work. To the Royal Shakespeare Company and its members Welcome!

Tim Supple, Artistic Director, Young Vic

This RSC/Allied Domecq Young Vic Season is, I think, both a measure of the RSC's current buoyancy and a recognition of the great success of last year's Stratford season. It will offer our audiences, many of whom will be familiar with the Young Vic from past transfers, a full new range of experiences in one of London's most exciting theatre spaces. The opening production of David Edgar's *Pentecost* is followed immediately by a fascinating pairing of two plays about Shakespeare's final days - his own last play *The Tempest* and Edward Bond's imaginative reconstruction *Bingo*. Our two companies will then work together on a new play, *Zenobia* by Nick Dear, direcred by Mike Okrent and the season ends with John Barton's acclaimed production of *Peer Gynt*, transferring from the Swan Theatre. We are delighted to be back at the Young Vic.

Adrian Noble Artistic Director, RSC

THE ROYAL SHAKESPEARE COMPANY

The Royal Shakespeare Company (RSC) is the title under which the Royal Shakespeare Theatre, Stratford-upon-Avon, has operated since 1961. Now one of the best known theatre companies in the world, the RSC builds on a long and distinguished history of theatre in Stratford-upon-Avon.

In essence, the aim of the Company is the same as that expressed in 1905 by Sir Frank Benson, then Director of the Stratford theatre: 'to train a company, every member of which would be an essential part of a homogeneous whole, consecrated to the practice of the dramatic arts and especially to the presentation of the plays of Shakespeare.' The RSC is formed around a core of Associate Artists - actors, directors, designers and others - with the aim that their different skills should combine, over the years, to produce a distinctive approach to theatre, both classical and modern.

The first permanent theatre in Stratford was built in 1879 but in 1926, just a year after the granting of its Royal Charter, this theatre was almost completely destroyed by fire. A worldwide campaign was launched to finance the building of a new one, and productions moved to a local cinema until the new theatre, designed by Elisabeth Scott, was opened by the Prince of Wales on 23 April 1932. Over the next thirty years, under the influence of directors such as Robert Atkins, William Bridges-Adams, Ben Iden Payne, Theodore Komisarjevsky, Sir Barry Jackson, Glen Byam Shaw and Anthony Quayle, the Shakespeare Memorial Theatre maintained a worldwide reputation.

In 1960, the newly-appointed Artistic Director, Peter Hall, extended the Company's operations to include a London base at the Aldwych Theatre, and widened the Company's repertoire to include modern as well as classical work. Other innovations of the period which have shaped today's Company were the travelling Theatre-go-round and experimental work which included the Theatre of Cruelty season.

Under Trevor Nunn, who took over as Artistic Director in 1968, this experimental work in small performance spaces led, in 1974, to the opening of The Other Place in Stratford, a studio theatre converted from a rehearsal room. In 1977 its London counterpart, The Warehouse, opened with a policy of presenting new British plays, and in the same year the RSC played its first season in Newcastle upon Tyne - now an annual event. In 1978, the year in which Terry Hands joined Trevor Nunn as Artistic Director, the RSC also fulfilled an ambition to tour towns and villages with little or no access to live professional theatre, a venture which has developed into the annual Regional Tour.

In 1982 the RSC moved its London base to the Barbican Centre in the City of London, opening both the Barbican Theatre, specially built for the RSC by the generosity of the City of London, and The Pit, a small theatre converted, like its predecessors, from a rehearsal space.

The 1986 season saw the opening of the Swan in Stratford. Built within the section of the shell of the Shakespeare Memorial Theatre which survived the 1926 fire, the Swan is a galleried playhouse staging the once hugely popular but now rarely seen plays of Shakespeare's contemporaries. Among other productions in the Swan, the RSC is engaged in a long-term exploration of the works of Shakespeare's two major contemporaries, Jonson and Marlowe. This new dimension to the Company's work was made possible by the extremely generous gift of a benefactor, Frederick R Koch. In early 1987 Terry Hands became sole Artistic Director and Chief Executive of the Company. He was succeeded as Artistic Director in July 1991 by Adrian Noble, supported by Michael Attenborough as Executive Producer and David Brierley as General Manager. The new Other Place opened under his leadership in the summer of 1991, built on the site of the original theatre with the aim of maintaining the tradition of studio theatre in Stratford, whilst pioneering in other areas. The Other Place now hosts overseas companies, workshops, teaching courses and conferences in all aspects of theatre, along with some of the Company's education work. It has also become the base for the annual Prince of Wales' Shakespeare School.

On 10 January 1994, the RSC announced a new £3.3 million record breaking sponsorship by Allied Domecq. This sponsorship will, amongst other activities, enable the RSC to undertake a regular international touring programme.

ROYAL SHAKESPEARE COMPANY

Patron
Her Majesty The Queen

President
His Royal Highness The Prince of Wales

Chairman of the Council Sir Geoffrey Cass

Vice-Chairmen Charles T Flower,
Professor Stanley Wells

DIRECTION

Artistic Director Adrian Noble

Executive Producer Michael Attenborough
General Manager David Brierley

Advisory Direction
John Barton, Peter Brook, Terry Hands,
Trevor Nunn

Emeritus Directors Trevor Nunn, Terry Hands

PRODUCERS

Lynda Farran *Acting Executive Producer*
Nicky Pallot *Producer*

ADMINISTRATION

Simon Bowler *Head of Technical Services*
Stephen Browning *Head of Marketing,
Press and Publicity*
David Fletcher *Head of Finance*
James Langley *Production Controller*
Carol Malcolmson *Planning Administrator*
Jonathan Pope *Development Director*
James Sargant *Administrator for Touring and
Special Projects*

HEADS OF DEPARTMENT

Angela Banks *Membership/Information*
Alan Bartlett *Construction*
Colin Chambers *Literary*
Alison Chard *Casting*
Susan Davenport *Sponsorship*
Kathy Elgin *Publications*
Wendy Greenhill *Education*
Andy Henson *Information Technology*
Tony Hill *Director of Projects*
Brenda Leedham *Wigs and Make-up*
William Lockwood *Property Shop*
Nigel Loomes *Paint Shop*
Chris Moody *Graphics*
Zoë Mylchreest *Press*
Ruth Sainsbury *Production Wardrobe*
Kevin Sivyer *Safety*
Andrew Wade *Voice*
John Watts *Management Services*
Guy Woolfenden *Music*

HISTORY

The Shakespeare Memorial Theatre opened
in 1879 and the theatre and company were re-named
'Royal Shakespeare' in 1961.
The Artistic Directors of the Royal Shakespeare Company
have been:

> Sir Peter Hall 1960-1968
> Trevor Nunn 1968-1978
> Trevor Nunn and Terry Hands 1978-1986
> Terry Hands 1986-1991
> Adrian Noble 1991-

The Royal Shakespeare Company is incorporated under
Royal Charter as The Royal Shakespeare Theatre,
Stratford-upon-Avon. Registered Charity No 212481

JOIN THE RSC MAILING LIST

For £6.00 a year you can join the RSC's mailing list as an
Associate Member for Stratford and Barbican theatres.
You receive:
• Advance information about performances at all RSC
theatres in Stratford and London, plus UK and overseas
tours, West End transfers and, for members in Scotland
and the northern counties, the RSC season in Newcastle
upon Tyne • Priority booking for performances in
Stratford, London and Newcastle where applicable •
Regular mailings throughout the year, including the RSC
Magazine • Members-only deferred payment facility •
Discounts on hotel accommodation at selected hotels in
Stratford.
Join now! Overseas and Student Group memberships (for
all educational organisations) are also available. You will
find application forms in the theatre foyers, or please
write, with SAE, to the Membership Office at the address
below.

STOP-OVER WITH THE RSC IN STRATFORD AND LONDON

The RSC's Stop-over packages combine a theatre ticket
with a pre- or after-show dinner and a choice of specially
selected hotel accommodation. The package operates in
both Stratford and London. For details and brochures,
please phone Shakespeare Stop-over on (01789) 414999.

For further details, please write to:
Royal Shakespeare Theatre, Stratford-upon-Avon,
Warwickshire, CV37 6BB. Telephone: (01789) 205301.

RSC COSTUME HIRE

Costumes from past RSC productions are available for
hire to other theatres, schools and amateur dramatic
societies. Enquiries to Karen Keene on 01789 205920.

TWENTY – FIVE YEARS
OF EXTRAORDINARY THEATRE
THE YOUNG VIC 1970 -1995

In 1968 Lord Olivier and the National Theatre (then based at the Old Vic) talked of a theatre which would form a centre of work particularly accessible to students and young people. The theatre's programme was to include the classics, new plays, experimental theatre and educational work.

The Young Vic was established in September 1970 and became the first major theatre producing work for younger audiences. In 1974 the Young Vic became independent of the National and went on to establish an international reputation for its productions, developing a wide-ranging audience of all ages and backgrounds.

Throughout its first twenty-five years, the Young Vic has created an enormous range and style of work, from Beckett to Sophocles and Shakespeare to Lennon, including the world premiere of *Joseph and the Amazing Technicolor Dreamcoat* (Tim Rice and Andrew Lloyd Webber), Tom Stoppard's *Rosencrantz and Guildenstern are Dead* and Arthur Miller's *The Last Yankee*. More recently, highly successful productions include Tim Supple's critically acclaimed *The Slab Boys Trilogy*, *Grimm Tales* and Theatre de Complicite's *The Street of Crocodiles*.

In its anniversary year, the Young Vic continues its commitment to creating adventurous theatre for as wide an audience as possible and particularly the young. As London's only theatre-in-the-round and most adaptable thrust stage, the Young Vic offers unique opportunities for the exploration of intimate ensemble performance and the imaginative use of space, light and sound.

The Young Vic aims to be equally known for its accessibility, as well as the creative and energetic way in which its work pursues the highest forms of artistic expression.

'Both the building and the stage/audience relationship are unique and altogether vital to the theatre scene of the metropolis'.
Trevor Nunn

YOUNG VIC COMPANY

The Young Vic gratefully acknowledges the financial assistance of the London Arts Board, the London Boroughs Grants Committee and the London Borough of Lambeth. Box Office sponsored by Digital.

Young Vic Company, 66 The Cut, Waterloo, London, SE1 8LZ. A company limited by guarantee, registered in England No. 1188209. VAT Registration No: 236 673348. Charity Registration No: 268876.

Box Office 0171 928 6363. Administration 0171 633 0133.
Press Office 0171 620 0568. Fax 0171 928 1585.

PENTECOST

DAVID EDGAR

This production is financially supported by **JBA**

CAST IN ORDER OF APPEARANCE

Oliver Davenport	Charles Kay
Gabriella Pecs	Jan Ravens
Teenage girl	Claire Carrie
Swedish man	Simon Cook
Fr Petr Karolyi	Nigel Cooke
Fr Sergei Bojovic	Roy Ward
Pusbas	Steven Elliott
Mikhail Czaba	Glenn Hugill
Leo Katz	Linal Haft
Anna Jedlikova	Judith Sweeney
Raif	Linford Brown
Antonio	Nigel Clauzel
Abdul	Quill Roberts
Yasmin	Katharine Rogers
Toni Newsome	Claire Carrie
Grigori Kolorenko	Sean O'Callaghan
Marina	Judith Sweeney
Cleopatra	Natalie Izgol/Rebecca Underwood
Amira	Catherine Kanter
Fatima	Sasha Behar
Nico	Steven Elliott
Tunu	Thusitha Jayasundera

Other parts played by members of the company

Directed by	Michael Attenborough
Designed by	Robert Jones
Lighting designed by	Robert A Jones
Music by	Ilona Sekacz
Research and Production Associate	Clarissa Brown
Movement by	Emma Rice
Translators and Foreign Language Advisers	Helen Rappaport and Kevin Smith
Sound by	Charles Horne
Accent Coach	Charmian Hoare

Fights by	Terry King
Company voice work by	Barbara Houseman and Andrew Wade
Stage Manager	Neil Constable
Deputy Stage Manager	Kate Vinnicombe/Nigel Pentland
Assistant Stage Manager	Deborah Gibbs

MUSICIANS

Keyboard Jonathan Rutherford
Choral music recorded by The Ambrosian Singers (Director John McCarthy)

The performance is approximately 3 hours in length,
including one interval of 15 minutes.

First performance of this production:
The Other Place, Stratford-upon-Avon, 12 October 1994.
First London performance: The Young Vic, 31 May 1995.

Please do not smoke or take cameras or tape recorders into the auditorium, and please remember that noise such as coughing, whispering, rustling or fanning programmes and the bleeping of digital watches can be distracting to the performers and also spoils the performance for other members of the audience.

In accordance with the requirements of the London Borough of Lambeth 'Persons shall not be permitted to stand or sit in any of the gangways. If standing be permitted in the gangways and at the rear of the seating, it shall be limited to the numbers indicated on notices exhibited in those positions'.

PRODUCTION ACKNOWLEDGEMENTS

Set construction by Robert Batchelor Scenery, rebuilt for the Young Vic by Simon Kenny, Souvenir Ltd. Scenic Artist Simon Kenny, Souvenir Ltd. Metalwork by John Wells of Binton Hill Forge. Painting, properties, costumes, wigs and make-up by RST Workshops, Stratford-upon-Avon. Properties Buyer Helen Skillicorn. Costume Supervisor Marina Montaut. Additional work on costumes by Glenda Sharpe. Linal Haft's outdoor clothing by Rohan. Thanks to Halina Boniszewska for Polish translation; to Tatiana Styrkas for Russian translation; and to Ivetta Mednikarova for Bulgarian translation. Thanks to Sharon Cather and Lisa Shekede of the Courtauld Institute for help and advice. Children's casting Adviser Janet Willis. Supernumerary Adviser Sam Jones. Production photographer: John Haynes.

Young Vic Season Co-ordinator: Denise Wood

PROGRAMME ACKNOWLEDGEMENTS

Books quoted from or consulted for this programme include: Northrop Frye, *Anatomy of Criticism*; EJ Hobsbawm, *Nations and Nationalism since 1780*, and Susan Richards, *Epics of Everyday Life*, Michael Baxandall: *Giotto and the Orators.* James Beck and Michael Daley: *Art Restoration*; David Talbot Rice: *Byzantine Art.*
Programme compiled by David Edgar and Kathy Elgin. Young Vic version edited by Alexandra Bannock. Front cover image: *Lamentation* (detail) by Giotto di Bondone. ©

MICHAEL ATTENBOROUGH

Director

THEATRE: Associate Director, Mercury Theatre, Colchester ('72 - '74). Associate Director, Leeds Playhouse ('74 - '79) - directed new plays by Willy Russell, Alan Bleasdale, James Robson and Arnold Wesker and classics by Chekhov, Shaw and Shakespeare. Associate Director, Young Vic ('79 - '80) - *What The Butler Saw, The Merchant of Venice*. Artistic Director, Palace Theatre Watford ('80 - '84) - productions include *The Girl in Melanie Klein, The Big Knife, Romantic Comedy* (also in the West End), *Terra Nova*. Artistic Director, Hampstead Theatre ('84 - '89) - productions include *The War at Home, Particular Friendships, That Summer, Observe the Sons of Ulster Marching Towards the Somme* (for which he won a Time Out Theatre Award), *Separation* (also in the West End). Hampstead won 23 major awards during his time there, with five productions transferring to the West End and one to Broadway, and in the 1987 Olivier Awards was nominated for the Observer Award for Outstanding Achievement. Artistic Director, The Turnstyle Group ('89 - '90) - *Over A Barrel, Single Spies*. Freelance work includes: *1984*, Citadel Theatre, Edmonton; *Yerma*, Abbey Theatre, Dublin; *Home Front*, Broadway; *Fashion*, Tricycle Theatre; *My Mother Said I Never Should*, Royal Court.

RSC: Executive Producer. Director: *Amphibians* (The Pit), *The Changeling* (Swan Theatre and The Pit), *Les Liaisons Dangereuses* (UK and European tour), *After Easter* (TOP and The Pit), *Pentecost* (TOP and Young Vic).

TELEVISION: BBC TV Drama Directors Course (1983). *The Importance of Being Earnest* (Channel 4).

SASHA BEHAR

Fatima

TRAINED: The Poor School.

THEATRE: *I Believe in Love* (Etcetera), Laida in *Madness in Valencia* (Gate Theatre, Notting Hill).

RSC: Perdita in *Tamburlaine the Great*. This season: Fatima in *Pentecost*.

TELEVISION: *Poirot's Christmas.*

CLARISSA BROWN

Research and Production Associate

BORN: Devon

TRAINED: Warwick University

THEATRE: As Director: *The Winter's Tale* (Devon Shakespeare Project); for Colway Theatre Trust *Out of the Blue, A Place Called Mars* (Co-Director), *Entertaining Strangers* (Assistant Director). *The Lover* (Battersea Arts Centre), *Riverman* (Tabard), *Leonce and Lena* (Warwick Arts Centre), *Angel City* (tour of Warwickshire), *The Odd Couple* (Hong Kong Arts Centre), *Tissue, Non Day Gun* (Hong Kong Fringe). Co-ordinated 1987 Hong Kong International Arts Festival.

RSC: Assistant Director on *Trolius and Cressida, Much Ado About Nothing, Richard II, Two Shakespearean Actors, The Strange Case of Dr Jekyll and Mr Hyde*. For RSC Fringe Festival directed *Leocadia*. This season: Research and Production Associate on *Pentecost*.

WRITING: *Shrimp Paste and Pearls, The Elfin Project.*

OTHER: Researcher on *Signals* (Channel 4), Reviewer for South China Morning Post and Hong Kong Standard. Currently producing research project about Hong Kong with National Life Story Collection at the British Library National Sound Archive.

LINFORD BROWN

Raif

BORN: Birmingham.

TRAINED: Webber Douglas.

THEATRE: Herostratus in *Forget Herostratus* (White Bear), *Clever Polly and the Stupid Wolf* (Polka), Jean in *Miss Julie* (Battersea Arts Centre), Brian in *Breakthrough* (Shaw). Tours UK: *Vibes from the Scribes* (Double Edge), Alfred in *Downside Up* (Act Theatre Co), *Maintrail* (Black Mime Theatre), Jean in *Miss Julie* (Pan Optic).

RSC: This season: Aedile in *Coriolanus*, Footman in *The Wives' Excuse*, Raif/2nd Soldier in *Pentecost*.

TELEVISION: *Only Fools and Horses.*

CLAIRE CARRIE

Toni Newsome/Teenage girl

TRAINED: St Andrew's University - MA (Hons), LAMDA.

THEATRE: Work at Northcott Theatre, Exeter: Geraldine in *What the Butler Saw*, Elizabeth-Jane in *The Mayor of Casterbridge*, Bianca in *The Taming of the Shrew*, Samantha in *The Magical Tales of the Brothers Grimm*.

RSC: This season: Melda in *After Easter*, Fanny in *The Wives' Excuse*, Toni in *Pentecost*.

NIGEL CLAUZEL

Antonio

BORN: London.

TRAINED: LAMDA.

THEATRE: Work at West Yorkshire Playhouse; Traverse Theatre, Edinburgh: Adam in *Someone Who'll Watch Over Me*, Paul in *Six Degrees of Separation*. Work in London: Mr Julian/Jacob in *Dizzy Heights* (Tabard Theatre).

RSC: This season: Aedile in *Coriolanus*, Footman in *The Wives' Excuse*, Antonio in *Pentecost*.

TELEVISION: *Between The Lines, The Bill, Burden of Proof.*

FILM: *The Young Americans.*

SIMON COOK
Swedish man

THEATRE: Work at Bristol Old Vic; Salisbury Playhouse; Mercury Theatre, Colchester: Steve Hubbel in *A Streetcar Named Desire*, Canon Throbbing in *Habeas Corpus*, Harry in *Not Now Darling*, Abanaza in *Aladdin*, Cubitt in *Brighton Rock*, Brian in *French Without Tears*, Sargeant Hayes in *Some Kind of Hero*, Bonario in *Volpone*, Albert Prosser in *Hobson's Choice*, Brodie in *The Real Thing*, Oliver Costello in *Spider's Webb*, Rodrigo in *The Duchess of Malfi*, Neville Strange in *Towards Zero*, Cleante in *Tartuffe*.

RSC: Sampson in *Romeo and Juliet*, Sir Henry Green in *Richard II*, The Wounded Man in *The Balcony*, Lord in *The Winter's Tale*. This season: Derek/Swedish man in *Pentecost*.

TELEVISION: *Devices and Desires*, *The Chief*, *London's Burning*, *Grange Hill*, *Watt on Earth*.

NIGEL COOKE
Father Karolyi

BORN: Dunkwa, Ghana.
TRAINED: Bristol Old Vic.
THEATRE: Extensive work at Bristol Old Vic, The Little Theatre Co. Bristol (of which he was a co-founder and director). Other regional work includes: *Playboy of the Western World*, *Getting Attention* (West Yorkshire Playhouse); *The Norman Conquests* (Windsor), *Time and Time Again*, *Serjeant Musgrave's Dance* (Scarborough), *A Man for all Seasons*, *Suddenly Last Summer* (Basingstoke), *Romeo and Juliet* (Bolton). Work in London: *The Duchess of Malfi* (Roundhouse), *The Public* (Theatre Royal Stratford East), *Having A Ball* (Lyric Hammersmith), *Serious Money* (Wyndham's), *The Recruiting Officer* (Royal Court), *Our Country's Good* (Royal Court and Garrick), *Caligula* (Boulevard), *Getting Attention* (Royal Court Theatre Upstairs).
RSC: Sebastian in *Twelfth Night*, Earl of Surrey in *Henry VIII*, Octavius in *Julius Caesar*, Bonario in *Volpone*, Tom Stone in *The School of Night*. This season: Nim/Montjoy in *Henry V*, Mr Wellvile in *The Wives' Excuse*, Father Karolyi in *Pentecost*.
TELEVISION: *Death of a Son*, *Galloping Galaxies*, *The Chief*, *Why Lockerbie?*, *The Bill*, *Hot Dog Wars*.
RADIO: *Dracula*.

DAVID EDGAR

THEATRE: Work includes *Excuses Excuses* (Belgrade Coventry 1972, Open Space 1973), *Dick Deterred* (Bush Theatre 1974), *Saigon Rose* (Traverse Edinburgh 1976), *Blood Sports* (Bush Theatre 1976), *Wreckers* (7:84 1977, *Teendreams* (with Susan Todd, Monstrous Regiment 1979), *Mary Barnes* (Birmingham Rep 1978, Royal Court 1979), *Entertaining Strangers* (Dorchester Community Play 1985, Cottesloe 1987), *That Summer* (Hampstead 1987), *The Shape of the Table* (Cottesloe 1990).
Work for the **RSC** includes: *Destiny* (1976), *The Jail Diary of Albie Sachs* (1978), *Nicholas Nickleby* (1980), *Maydays* (1983), *The Strange Case of Dr Jekyll and Mr Hyde* (1991). This season: *Pentecost*.
TELEVISION: Includes *Baby Love*, *Destiny*, *The Jail Diary of Albie Sachs*, *Nicholas Nickleby*, *Vote For Them*, *Buying A Landslide*, *Citizen Locke*.
RADIO: Includes *Ecclesiastes*, *Saigon Rose*, *A Movie Starring Me*, *That Summer*.
FILM: *Lady Jane*.

STEVEN ELLIOTT
Pusbas/Nico

TRAINED: Welsh College of Music and Drama.
THEATRE: Seasons at Salisbury, Cardiff, Leatherhead. Florizel in *The Winter's Tale*, Ventocello in *Amadeus*, Mr Elton in *Emma*, Player King/Osric in *Hamlet*, Marquis/Attourney General in *A Tale of Two Cities*, Double-O-Rodge in *Never Say Never...Ever!* (Edinburgh and Old Red Lion), Roy in *Lone Star*.
RSC: Chiron in *Titus Andronicus*, Pilia Borza in *The Jew of Malta*, Les Epsom in *Bite of the Night*, Junior in *The Revenger's Tragedy*, Trebonius in *Julius Caesar*, The Soldier in *Principia Scriptoria*, Angelo's Servant in *Measure for Measure*. This season: Antonio in *Twelfth Night*, Earl of Cambridge/Gower in *Henry V*, Pusbas in *Pentecost*. RSC Fringe: *Words Words Words* (poetry antology compiled by Cicely Berry and Andrew Wade), Erwin Forrester in *Redskin*.
TELEVISION: *Inspector Morse*, *Van der Valk*, *That Uncertain Feeling*.

LINAL HAFT
Leo Katz

BORN: Leeds.
THEATRE: Work at Leicester Haymarket; Coventry; Bristol Old Vic; Theatre Royal, Northampton; The Coliseum, Oldham; Leeds Playhouse; Birmigham Rep; Nuffield Theatre, Southampton; Arts Theatre, Cambridge; Young Lyceum, Edinburgh Festival; Library Theatre, Manchester: Title role in *Macbeth*, Macheath in *The Threepenny Opera*, Arnold in *Torch Song Trilogy*, Bottom in *A Midsummer Night's Dream*, Jean in *Miss Julie*, The Corporal in *The Caucasian Chalk Circle*, Potiphar in *Joseph and the Amazing Technicolor Dreamcoat*, Aristotle Onassis in *Callas*, Sammy Samuels in *Comedians*, Philip Marlowe in *Private Dick*, Mo Axelrod in *Awake and Sing*, the King in *The King and I*, Lenny in *The Homecoming*, Dame in *Dick Whittington*, Otto in *Through the Leaves*, Leahy in *Safe in Our Hands*. Work in London: Bill Sikes in *Oliver!* (West End and Toronto, Canada), Groucho Marx in *Groucho in Toto*, Ali Hakim in *Oklahoma!*, Groucho Marx in *Minnies Boys*, Girli in *Arturo Ui* (West End), *Edmond* (Royal Court), The Father in *After The Fall*, Tamazo in *The Changeling* (RNT) Man in *Lunch* (Young Vic Studio), Alain in *The School For Wives* (Almeida).
RSC: This season: Fluellen/French Ambassador in *Henry V*, Sicinius Velutus in *Coriolanus*, Leo in *Pentecost*.
TELEVISION: *The Charmer*, *Bust*, *Remington Steele*, *Shine*

on *Harvey Moon, Matlock, First Among Equals, Minder, Ball Trap on the Côte Sauvage, Night of the Golden Brain, Comedians, Great Expectations, Without Walls: The Great Dictator.*

FILM: *The Birth of the Beatles, Zero Option, Minder on the Orient Express, Excape from Sobibor.*

OTHER: Features on Pete Townshend's *Psychoderilict* album and toured the USA with the stage version iast summer.

CHARMIAN HOARE
Dialect Coach

THEATRE: *The Children's Hour, The Dark at the Top of the Stair, Touched, Arsenic and Old Lace, Tokens of Affection* (Derby Playhouse), *All My Sons, The Crucible, Winding the Ball, The Odd Couple, The Glass Menagerie* (Manchester Royal Exchange), *The Plough and the Stars* (Banff Centre for the Arts, Canada), *Steel Magnolias, From the Mississippi Delta* (Talawa Theatre Company), *Street Scene* (ENO), *All My Sons* (Salisbury Playhouse).

RSC: *The Wizard of Oz, Kiss Me Kate, Two Shakespearean Actors.* Voice Coach in Stratford 1991-92. Dialect Coach for *The Merry Wives of Windsor, Misha's Party, King Baby, Travesties, Unfinished Business, The Venetian Twins, Elgar's Rondo, New England.* This season: *After Easter, Pentecost, The Devil is an Ass, The Taming of the Shrew, The Relapse.*

GLENN HUGILL
Mikhail Czaba

BORN: Durham.

TRAINED: Webber Douglas Academy of Dramatic Art.

THEATRE: Leon Czolgosz in *Assassins*, Paul in *Elegies* (Manchester Library Theatre). Work in London: Doug in *Six Degrees of Separation* (Royal Court/West End), Sigismund in *Life's A Dream* (White Bear). Tours Abroad: Aston in *The Caretaker* (London City Theatre, Vienna).

RSC: This season: Valentine in *Twelfth Night*, Courtall's Footman in *The Wives' Excuse*, Mikhail Czaba in *Pentecost*.

TELEVISION: *Just a Gigolo, The Upper Hand, Chandler and Co.*

RADIO: *King's Rhapsody, Loose Ends, Jane and Prudence, Shatterhand.*

OTHER: Improvised comedy live and for the BBC.

THUSITHA JAYASUNDERA
Tunu

TRAINED: RADA.

THEATRE: First work in theatre.

RSC: This season: Anitra/Huhu in *Peer Gynt*, Gentlewoman in *Coriolanus*, Tunu in *Pentecost*.

TELEVISION: *Firm Friends, The All New Alexei Sayle Show.*

ROBERT JONES
Designer

Robert Jones graduated from the Central School of Art and Design. He has been Head of Design at Newcastle Playhouse, Nottingham Playhouse and most recently from 1990 to 1992 he was Head of Design at the newly built West Yorkshire Playhouse where his designs included *Wild Oats, Carousel, The Maple Tree Game, What Every Woman Knows* and *Playboy of the Western World.* Freelance design credits include *Private Lives, Look Back in Anger* (Bristol Old Vic), *Henry IV Part 1, Macbeth* (Newcastle), *A Midsummer Night's Dream* (Nottingham), *The Secret Rapture* (Los Angeles - Drama-Logue Critics Award for Best Scenic Design), *Colours* (Abbey Theatre, Dublin), *Getting Attention* (Royal Court), *Bold Girls, Back Up The Hearse and Let Them Smell The Flowers* (Hampstead); national tours of *Salt of the Earth* and *Happy Families.* In the West End, Robert Jones has designed *Rosencrantz and Guildenstern are Dead* (Piccadilly), *The Pope and the Witch* (Comedy), *April in Paris* (Ambassadors), *The Prime of Miss Jean Brodie* (Strand). Most recent work inludes: *Romeo and Juliet, Dangerous Corner, Rope* (Birmingham Rep), *All God's Chillun Got Wings, Someone To Watch Over Me* (West Yorkshire Playhouse), *Democracy* (Bush), *A Collier's Friday Night* (Hampstead).

ROBERT A JONES
Lighting Designer

Technical director The Other Place. Most recent work includes:

RSC: *King John, King Lear, The Odyssey.* This season: *Moby Dick, After Easter, Transit of Venus, Pentecost.*

OPERA: *King Priam, L'ajo, Nell'Imbarazzo* (Batignano), *Beauty and the Beast, Zaide , Les Boreades, Faust* (City of Birmingham Touring Opera).

Other work includes design and consultancy for many trade exhibitions, conferences and product launches, both in this country and abroad.

CATHERINE KANTER
Amira

BORN: London.

STUDIED: University of East Anglia.

TRAINED: Mountview Theatre School.

THEATRE: Clarice in *The Servant of Two Masters* (West Yorkshire Playhouse and the International Goldoni Festival in Italy).

RSC: This season: Helga/Cook in *Peer Gynt*, Mrs Woudmore's Page in *The Wives' Excuse*, Amira/Restorer in *Pentecost*.

CHARLES KAY
Oliver Davenport

TRAINED: RADA. Winner Bancroft Gold Medal.
THEATRE: London West End includes: Jimmy Beales in *Roots*, The Pope in *Luther*, Magpie in *The Naked Island*, Clincher in *The Constant Couple*, Dauphin in *St Joan*, Sam in *The Homecoming*, Egyptian Doctor in *The Millionairess*, Chauvelin in *The Scarlet Pimpernel*, Mr Kipps in *The Woman in Black*. Work for the RNT: Gaveston in *Edward II*, Celia in *As You Like It*, Sir Nathaniel in *Love's Labour's Lost*, Loach in *The National Health*, Arrogon in *The Merchant of Venice*, Solyoni in *The Three Sisters*, The Elderly Gentleman in *Back To Methusela*, Robespeirre in *Danton's Death*, Harphgon in *The Miser*, Dr Willis in *The Madness of George III*.
RSC: Octavius in *Julius Caesar*, Clarence in *The Wars of the Roses*, Navarre in *Love's Labour's Lost*, Launcelot Gobbo in *The Merchant of Venice*, Anipholus of Syracuse in *The Comedy of Errors*, Dubchinski in *The Government Inspector*, Osric in *Hamlet*, Moloch in *Baron Bolligrew*, Basilio in *Life's A Dream*, Lord Canteloupe in *Waste* (Clarence Derwent Award). This season: Oliver in *Pentecost*.
TELEVISION: Includes *The Duchess of Malfi, Fall of Eagles, Loyalties, To Serve Them All My Days, My Cousin Rachel, The Edge of Darkness, Fortunes of War, Fiddlers Three, Law and Disorder.*
FILM: Includes *Nijinski, Amadeus, Henry V, The Heart of Darkness.*

TERRY KING
Fight Director

THEATRE: *King Lear, The Murderers, Fool For Love,* (RNT), *Oleanna, Search and Destroy, Sore Throats* (Royal Court), *Othello, Hamlet, Romeo and Juliet* (Bristol Old Vic).
RSC: *Hamlet* (NatWest tour 1987), *Pericles, Singer, Troilus and Cressida., As You Like It, Richard III, Julius Caesar.* This season: *Henry V, Coriolanus, Twelfth Night, Romeo and Juliet, The Devil is an Ass.*
OPERA: *Otello* (WNO), *Porgy and Bess* (Glyndebourne), *West Side* Story (York), *Carmen* (ENO).
TELEVISION: *Fell Tiger, A Kind of Innocence, A Fatal Inversion, The Bill, EastEnders.*

SEAN O'CALLAGHAN
Grigori Kolorenko

TRAINED: RADA.
THEATRE: Work at the New Vic Theatre, Stoke-on-Trent: George Deever in *All My Sons*, Dr McFarlane in *Hobson's Choice*, Mulvaney in *Soldiers Three, Eric The Epic*, Brian Davies in *The Dirty Hill*, Jack Clitheroe in *The Plough and the Stars*, Sir Andrew Aguecheek in *Twelfth Night*, Casca in *Julius Caesar*, Captain Phoebus de Chanterpeaurs in *The Hunchback of Notre Dame*, Jim Rhys in *The Bright and Bold Design*. Work in London: Gummery in *The Bite of the Night* (Almeida), Reb Gediliya in *Satan in Goray* (New End).
RSC: Gregory/Peter in *Romeo and Juliet*, Bishop of Carlisle in *Richard II*, Dion in *The Winter's Tale, Country Dancing*, Shapkin in *The Storm*. RSC Festivals: Iron in *Class Enemy*, Adonis in *Venus and Adonis*. This season: Clarence/M. le fer in *Henry V*, Paul Watterson in *After Easter*, Grigori in *Pentecost*.
TELEVISION: *Medics, Casualty, The Last Romantics.*
FILM: *The Long Shot.*

JAN RAVENS
Gabriella Pecs

BORN: Merseyside.
STUDIED: Homerton College, Cambridge.
THEATRE: Work at Chichester, Watford, Birmingham: Hoyden in *The Relapse*, Sophia in *Tom Jones*, Judy in *Middle Age Spread*, Viola in *Twelfth Night*. Work in London: *Sloane Ranger Revue* (Duchess Theatre). Tours UK: Stand-up comedy around colleges, universities and London circuit. Tour abroad: Ruth in Pete Townshend's *Psychoderelict* (USA and Canada).
RSC: This season: Ermer/Elish in *After Easter*, Gabriella in *Pentecost*.
TELEVISION: Includes *The Lenny Henry Show, Friday People, The Kenny Everett Show, An Actor's Life For Me, B and B, Carrott's Lib, Spitting Image, Cats Eyes, No Frills, Alexei Sayle's Stuff, Whose Line Is It Anyway?, Have I Got News For You, One Foot in the Grave, The Final Frame, Luv, Alas Smith and Jones, Fireworks, Harry Enfield and Chums.*
RADIO: *Brunch, The Uncyclopaedia of Rock, Week-Ending, 3+1, Loose Ends, Just A Minute, Midweek, Womans Hour, Any Other Business, Wodehouse Playhouse, Womens Troubles, Looking Forward to the Past, Wordly Wise.*
RECORDING: *Psychoderelict* (album).

EMMA RICE
Movement

TRAINED: Guildhall School of Music and Drama; Gardzienice Theatre Association, Poland.
MOVEMENT/CHOREOGRAPHY: *They Shoot Horses Don't They?, The Swan* (Northern Stage, Newcastle), *Tess of the d'Urbervilles* (West Yorkshire Playhouse, Leeds), *Women of Troy* and *The House of Bernarda Alba* (The Gate, London), *The Lucky Chance* (Derby Playhouse), *Goatsong, Birthday* (Theatre Alibi).
AS A PERFORMER: Extensive work with Theatre Alibi and Kneehigh Theatre, Cornwall. Other work includes: Chorus Leader in *Women of Troy*, Amelia in *The House of Bernarda Alba*, Susan in *Arden of Faversham* (Classics on a Shoestring, Gate Theatre, London). Work abroad: *Carmina Burana* (Gardzienice Theatre Association, Poland).
RSC: Movement for *A Woman Killed With Kindness*. This season: *Pentecost, The Taming of the Shrew.*

QUILL ROBERTS

Abdul

BORN: London.
TRAINED: Birmingham School of Speech and Drama.
THEATRE: Work at Grand Theatre, Wolverhampton; Belgrade Theatre, Coventry: Pau-Puk-Keewis in *Hiawatha*, Marcus Steel in *Contenders* (Theatre Absolute). Tybalt in *Romeo and Juliet* (Tour with Soapbox).
RSC: This season: Bates/Berri in *Henry V*, Footman in *The Wives' Excuse*, Abdul in *Pentecost*.

KATHARINE ROGERS

Yasmin

BORN: London.
TRAINED: RADA.
THEATRE: Work at Traverse Theatre, Edinburgh; Liverpool Playhouse; Contact Theatre, Manchester; Crucible Theatre, Sheffield; Derby Playhouse, Birmingham Rep: Kay in *Fugue*, Gilda in *Design for Living*, Lily/Nina in *The Seagull*, Isabella in *Measure for Measure*, Stage Manager in *Our Town*, Frankie in *Frankie and Johnny*, Helen in *Action Replay*, Castabella in *The Atheist's Tragedy*, Jocasta in *Oedipus Tyrannus*. Work in London: Blanche in *The Piggy Bank* (Greenwich), Kate in *The Pool at Bethesda* (Orange Tree), Guenevere in *Morte D'Arthur* (Lyric Hammersmith). Tours UK: Viola in *Twelfth Night*, Antigone in *The Oedipus Trilogy* (Oxford Playhouse Co.), Amanda in *A Slight Hangover* (Bromley), Alice in *The Voysey Inheritance* (Lyceum, Edinburgh). Directed: *1953* (Greenwich Studio Theatre).
RSC: Helena in *A Midsummer Night's Dream*, Paris' Page in *Romeo and Juliet* (Small Scale Tour), Pauline in *Golden Girls*, Marie in *Red Noses*, Janine in *Camille*, Cant in *The Castle*, Sister Mary Joseph in *Today*, Trellis in *Crimes in Hot Countries*, Milanka in *The Party*. RSC Festivals: *After the Assissinations*, *Freedom in not a Breakfast Food*. This season: Helen in *After Easter*, Mrs Sightly in *The Wives' Excuse*, Yasmin in *Pentecost*.
TELEVISION: *Bloody Kids*, *Only Yesterday*, *London's Burning*, *The Bill*, *Yo Picasso*.
FILM: *Quadrophenia*, *London's Burning*.
RADIO: *The Pool at Bethesda*.

ILONA SEKACZ

Composer

THEATRE: Includes *A Handful of Dust*, *La Ronde* (Shared Experience), *A Patriot For Me* (Haymaket), *The Glass Menagerie* (Greenwich), *Major Barbara*, *Saint Joan*, *The Real Inspector Hound*, *The Critic*, *The Cherry Orchard*, *Countrymania*, *Cat on a Hot Tin Roof*, *The Secret Rapture*, *Bartholomew Fair* (RNT).
RSC: *King Lear*, *Twelfth Night*, *Henry VIII*, *Measure for Measure*, *The Merchant of Venice*, Bond's *Lear*, *Golden Girls*, *Troilus and Cressida*, *Les Liaisons Dangereuses* (London and Broadway), *Mephisto*, *The Danton Affair*, *Cymbeline*, *The Jew of Malta*, *Indigo*, *A Question of Geography*, *The Man of Mode*, *Restoration*, *Cymbeline*, *Across Oka*, *The Love of the Nightingale*, *As You Like It*, *Dr Faustus*, *A Midsummer Night's Dream*, *Singer*, *Much Ado About Nothing*, *Edward II*, *Twelfth Night*, *Romeo and Juliet*, *The Thebans*, *The Beggar's Opera*, *The Odyssey*, *Antony and Cleopatra*, *The School of Night*. This season: *A Midsummer Night's Dream*, *Pentecost*.
TELEVISION: Includes *Boys From the Blackstuff*, *Freud*, *Bluebell*, *The Insurance Man*, *Northanger Abbey*, *Hedgehog Wedding*, *Rat in the Skull*, *The Importance of Being Earnest*, *Intimate Contact*, *The Final Run*, *The Picnic*, *The Justice Game*, *Back Home*, *The Heat of the Day*, *Traitors*, *The Common Pursuit*, *Redemption*, *Love On A Branch Line*.
FILM: *A Pin for the Butterfly*.
RADIO: Includes *Romeo and Juliet*, *Cymbeline*, *Macbeth*, *Richard II*, *Oedipus*, *Dreamplay*, *Tom Jones*, *Kipps*, *Peter Grimes*.
OPERA: *A Small Green Space* (ENO Baylis programme).
BALLET: *The Queue* (English Dance Theatre).

JUDITH SWEENEY

Marina/Anna Jedlikova

TRAINED: RSAMD.
THEATRE: Work at Traverse Theatre, Lyceum Theatre, Edinburgh; Cumbernauld Theatre; Tron Theatre, Citizen's Theatre, Glasgow: Gertrude Twine in *Rookery Nook*, Belinda Blair in *Noises Off*, Marcelle in *Little Hotel on the Side* Grudrun Ensslin in *Ulrikie*, Laura in *The Glass Menagerie*, Alice in *Who's Left*, Red in *Exercise in Primary Colours*, Dora Cant in *Mrs Murray's Baby*, Mrs Candour in *The School For Scandal*, Dorine in *Tartuffe*. Work in London: Vassa (Gate Theatre, Notting Hill), Doris in *For His Namesake*, Dolly in *Dolorosa*, Jinty in *D'Mon Get Aff* (Arches Theatre), Margaret in *The Talk of the Steamie* (Greenwich), Fleas in *The Magic Snowball*, Gerda in *The Snow Queen*, Mary in *Whittington*, Gwen in *Merlin the Magnificent*. Tours: Pauline Graham in *Through The Wall*; Nerissa in *The Merchant of Venice* (Vanessa Ford), *The Hollow Crown* (Swaive Kinoozier); For 7:84 Theatre Company: Ellen in *Screw the Bobbin*, Beatrice in *Women in Power*, Mary in *Johnny Noble*, Isa in *Men Should Weep*.
RSC: This season: Anna Jedlikova/Marina in *Pentecost*, Queen Isabel/ Governor of Harfleur in *Henry V*.
TELEVISION: *Childrens' Ward*, *Growing Pains*, *The Bill* *The Conversion of St Paul*, *Take the High Road*, *A Christmas Village*, *Taggart*, *Maureen Reid*, *Where Are You?*, *Brookside* *YES*, *Biting The Hand*, *Scotch and Rye*.
FILM: *Tom and Viv*.

ROY WARD

Father Bojovik

BORN: Richmond-on-Thames.
THEATRE: Recently: *Mandragola* (Southwark Playhouse) *The Duchess of Malfi* (DOC). Tour UK: *A Christmas Carol*.
RSC: This season: Understudy in *Peer Gynt*, Campbell Commanding Officer in *After Easter*, Father Brojovik Commander in *Pentecost*.

THE RSC/ALLIED DOMECQ YOUNG VIC SEASON

FROM 31 MAY
Pentecost
by David Edgar
Directed by Michael Attenborough

FROM 14 JUNE
The Tempest
by William Shakespeare
Directed by David Thacker

FROM 21 JUNE
Bingo
by Edward Bond
Directed by David Thacker

FROM 2 AUGUST
Zenobia
by Nick Dear
Directed by Mike Okrent

FROM 31 AUGUST
Peer Gynt
by Henrik Ibsen
in a version by John Barton
based on the text by Christopher Fry,
with lyrics by Adrian Mitchell
Directed by John Barton

"I thought Shakespeare would be dead boring. Now I know about the story, I can see that there are things that relate to your own life. What Shakespeare says still means something now."

Young people taking part in RSC workshops are learning that Shakespeare is as relevant today as 400 years ago.

It's not just a lesson for children.

Brave new worlds can open up for adults too as they discover the passion and excitement of Shakespeare's works in live performance.

That is why, as the principal sponsor of the RSC, the international drinks and retailing group Allied Domecq is working in partnership with the RSC to help spread the word about Shakespeare throughout the world.

Horizons are expanding for the RSC as Allied Domecq's sponsorship is enabling it to extend its international touring programme taking its world class productions to new audiences in more countries than ever before.

Together, Allied Domecq and the RSC are encouraging more people to experience and enjoy live theatre, including works by modern playwrights as well as those of Shakespeare.

RSC

ROYAL
SHAKESPEARE
COMPANY

Sponsored by
ALLIED
DOMECQ

Allied Domecq trades in over 150 countries providing drinks, food, hospitality and enjoyment around the world.
***Allied Domecq Spirits & Wine** is the world's second largest spirits company, with 13 of the world's top brands including Ballantine's, Kahlua, Beefeater, Canadian Club, Courvoisier and Presidente.*
***Allied Domecq Retailing** is the world's fourth largest retailer. Its 13,000 outlets include Dunkin' Donuts and Baskin-Robbins.*

RSC Education Officer Dominic Gray in a workshop with a pupil from Eastbury School, Barking, England, June 1994.
Photo: Allan Titmuss

It is ordained by Nature that nothing should be able to progress or grow very much that is not being built up, elaborated and refined by many individual men, particularly men who are in competition with each other and vying with each other for public esteem . . . Just as no city, so also no art can be established by a single man, nor indeed by a few men; it needs many, very many men, and these men must not be unknown to each other – how otherwise could they vie with each other and contend for glory? But above all else they must be known and related to each other by virtue of communication in the same language. I have already taken a simile from the building of a city: do we not also learn from the Bible that the men who built the great tower of Babel stopped building it precisely because they did not fully understand each other's speech?

> *Lorenzo Valla, fifteenth-century art critic,*
> *quoted in Michael Baxandall,*
> *Giotto and the Orators*

Gentlemen, Europe has so far only taken pictures of Muslim women wearing veils who have walked 40 kilometres, who are hungry and tired. So the world is afraid of them as anyone would be. I would just like to show you what the modern Bosnian Muslim woman looks like. She is a citizen of Europe, whether Europe wishes to accept it or not.

> *Nadja Ridic (self-described as a typical atheist*
> *Bosnian Muslim), BBC Everyman, April 1993*

All those things you experienced in Western Europe – the Renaissance, the Reformation, the eighteenth-century Enlightenment and constitutionalism – all these were things we missed because of the Turks.

> *Sofia University official,*
> *The Guardian, 15 February 1991*

To Mike

Acknowledgments

I am indebted to Helen Rappaport and Kevin Smith who translated and taught the European and Middle Eastern languages, and to Thusitha Jayasundera who translated and spoke the Sinhalese. For the story-telling scene as a whole, I owe much to the company and to Clarissa Brown, with whom the scene was created in rehearsal .

For research help and advice I am grateful to Sharon Cather of the Courtauld Institute, Christopher Frayling of the Royal College of Art, Paul Joannides of the University of Cambridge and Nigel Llewellyn of the University of Sussex; to Rotraut Lippke, Vayu Naidu, Hilary Norrish, Tom Phillips, Giles Quarme and Susan Richards; and to the staff of the British Council, the Institute of Race Relations, and Statewatch.

D.E.

PENTECOST

Characters

GABRIELLA Pecs, *art curator*
OLIVER Davenport, *art historian*
Father Sergei BOJOVIC, *Orthodox*
Father Petr KAROLYI, *Catholic*
Mikhail CZABA, *minister*
PUSBAS, *leader of Heritage*
LEO Katz, *art historian*
Anna JEDLIKOVA, *former dissident*
TONI Newsome, *TV hostess*

A teenage GIRL
A SWEDISH MAN
FIRST SOLDIER
SECOND SOLDIER
Czaba's SECRETARY
A RESTORER
A POLICEWOMAN
A DRIVER
FIRST COMMANDO
SECOND COMMANDO

YASMIN, *Palestinian Kuwaiti*
RAIF, *Azeri*
ANTONIO, *Mozambican*
AMIRA, *Bosnian*
MARINA, *Russian*
GRIGORI, *Ukrainian*
ABDUL, *Afghan*
TUNU, *Sri Lankan*
NICO, *'Bosnian' Roma*
CLEOPATRA, *'Bosnian' Roma*
FATIMA, *Kurd*

Restorers, Soldiers, Commandos

Location

The play is set in an abandoned church of the Romanesque period in an unnamed south-east European country. The large main door is to one side; facing us is an imposing wall, on which a large heroic revolutionary mural has been painted. There is also a high window through which it is possible to monitor the approach to the main door. There is at the beginning a stage spotlight, a stepladder covered in curtaining, and other debris attesting to the church's chequered history.

The fresco that is discovered behind the mural is only seen in total at the very end: in Scene One a small section is revealed, in Scene Two it is in the process of being cleaned, in Scene Three it is being covered with a gauze and canvas facing, a procedure completed by Scene Four. In the second act, the facing is removed but the painting remains largely in darkness until the beginning of Scene Seven. We do however see reproductions and outlines of sections of the painting, and the whole in a blown up photograph.

Although stylistically Byzantine, the painting is compositionally clearly very similar to Giotto's Lamentation in the Arena Chapel, Padua (the main iconographic differences are described in the text). It is important that the section revealed in Scene One includes foreshortening, elements of perspective and clearly solid figures.

Language

All characters speak the languages they know, whether their own or indeed English. For information, I have identified the languages and given English translations of the non-English speeches (printed in square brackets and not intended to be spoken).

In this text, the non-Roman script languages are phonetically transliterated, as is the Polish (in round brackets between the correctly-spelt speech and the English translation). The language of 'our country' is in fact Bulgarian, though Bulgaria is not 'our country'.

The transliteration is intended to render the languages in a form that will be accessible to actors, to convey the equivalent sounds of the letters rather than their correct orthography.

In the case of the Arabic and Turkic speeches, there are a number of vowels and consonants which have no direct equivalent in English. Thus 'aa', 'ee' and 'oo' are long (as in *far*, *been* and *pool*); 'o' is like the vowel in *third*, 'u' is like the *tu* in French, and the vowel 'ı' is like the 'er' in *father*. 'kh' is like the 'ch' in *loch*, 'H' is a strongly aspirated 'h', 'gh' like the French 'r' in *Paris*, 'q' is similar to a hard C, ''' is a glottal stop, and 'c' is a kind of choke, with no equivalent in English.

ACT ONE

The primary purpose of the painter is to
make a plane surface display a body
in relief, detached from the plane,
and he who in that art most surpasses
others deserves most praise.

Leonardo da Vinci

What determines and characterises European culture? Europe is formed by the community of nations which are largely characterised by the inherited civilisation whose most important sources are: the Judao-Christian religion, the Greek-Hellenistic ideas in the field of government, philosophy, arts and science, and finally, the Roman views concerning law.

Mr M. Mourik, Dutch ambassador
for International Cultural Cooperation, 1987

For more than a generation we have been bombarded with jingles and ditties about 'whiter than white' laundry, sparkling pots and pans, glistening floors, glowing toilet bowls. It is the same with our bodies: our hair, shimmering, dyed a designer-selected colour, our teeth capped pearly white. We must be scrubbed and caressed with chemicals, and covered again with fragrances and Fomblin-like oils, our faces lifted and lumpy cellulite made to disappear with miraculous products.

The treatment of art was not immune to this obsession with perfection. For if clean is beautiful, dirty is ugly, dirty is poor and dirty is bad. Get it off, get it all off. Brush a chemical on, let it work and wipe it away. That is how Easy-off gets the grime from the stove, and that is how AB57 works. No ring around the collar, no telltale stains . . .

As I stand against pollution of our world so do I oppose the risky restoration of the Sistine ceiling.

James Beck, art historian, in Art Restoration

All I know is that it's about three sides and this cleansing thing.

Samantha Fox, on a visit to Bosnia, 7 July 1993

ACT ONE

Scene One

Autumn. The church at night. Shafts of moonlight through high windows; the arc of car headlamps from a nearby motorway curl through the open door. An Englishman between 40 and 50 stands amid the debris. Nearby is a Woman with a torch, in her 30s, a native of this country. They are both dressed smartly, though not formally, for dinner; they both wear overcoats and scarves. He is OLIVER DAVENPORT, an art historian; she is GABRIELLA PECS, of the National Museum.

OLIVER. So this is it?

    GABRIELLA *nods.*

This is the place?

    GABRIELLA *nods.*

Where are we?

GABRIELLA. Okeydoke.

    She goes to shut the main door, blocking most of the light from the cars and the traffic noise.

Hang on one moment.

OLIVER (*to himself*). 'Okeydoke'.

    Seeing her shut the door, glancing at his watch.

I do – you know, I have this dinner.

GABRIELLA. Yeah, yeah. I attend it.

OLIVER. I address it. May I ask –

    GABRIELLA *finds the light and turns it on.*

GABRIELLA. Voilà.

    The light illuminates the grand heroic revolutionary picture on the wall.

OLIVER. Good lord. The heroic revolutionary masses.

GABRIELLA. Plus naturally allies in cooperative peasantry and forward-viewing technical intelligensia.

    GABRIELLA *takes the curtaining off the ladder in order to climb up the wall.*

OLIVER. Presumably that's 'forward-looking'.

GABRIELLA. Towards radiant future in which everybody's quite as primitive and backwards clods as everybody else.

OLIVER. Now look, I really ought to –

GABRIELLA. Illyich.

Slight pause.

OLIVER. I'm sorry?

GABRIELLA. You ask where we are. Answer: filthy little village, 20 kilometres off capital, and 17 off border.

OLIVER. Illyich?

GABRIELLA. It is Lenin's father's name.

OLIVER. I know. I wondered why they hadn't changed it back.

GABRIELLA. Smart question. Unfortunately villagers cannot agree new name. Historic name, for Hungarians is Cholovar, for Saxons Klozendorf, for rest of people Clop.

OLIVER *laughs.*

This is amusing?

OLIVER. No. No, I was only thinking: just one vowel shift, and I'd be stranded miles from anywhere, about to miss a professionally vital dinner in the presence of your Minister of Culture and His Excellency the Ambassador, in the abandoned Church of St Pulcheria the Pious, Clap.

GABRIELLA. It is church of St John Climacus, actually. And he is now called Minister for Restoration of our National Monuments. And what is so desperately funny about a village means 'applause'?

OLIVER. Well, nothing, obviously. It's just that, as it happens, um, colloquially . . .

GABRIELLA. Yes?

OLIVER. 'Clap' means VD. Venereal, – uh, sexual disease.

Slight pause.

GABRIELLA. I see.

OLIVER. In fact, 'clop' means a – the sound of horse's hooves.

GABRIELLA (*trying it out*). Clop, clop.

OLIVER. Clip clop.

GABRIELLA (*affecting 'all the difference'*). *Clip* clop.

OLIVER. Yes.

GABRIELLA *climbs up the ladder.*

GABRIELLA. As it happens you're not stranded. You will be back for your important dinner in good time.

OLIVER. That's a relief.

GABRIELLA. But now dear Dr Davenport five minutes please.

    Pause.

OLIVER. It took the best part of an –

GABRIELLA. I drive roundabout. Will you take bricks please?

    Pause.

    Five minutes only. Please.

    OLIVER *can't not help as* GABRIELLA *begins to take bricks out of the cooperative peasantry.*

OLIVER. Okeydoke.

    GABRIELLA *handing bricks down.*

GABRIELLA. All righty, one abandoned church. As well as ware-house, church is used by heroic peasantry for store potatoes. *Pile* bricks please. And before potatoes, Museum of Atheism and Progressive People's Culture. And before museum, prison.

OLIVER. Prison?

    OLIVER *is taking the bricks.* GABRIELLA *is revealing a section of dirty whitewashed wall with scribbled words on it.*

GABRIELLA. 'Transit Centre'. German Army. You can still see signatures of prisoners on wall. You note also wall is whitewash with clear mark of nail where Catholics hang pictures, how you say it, Via Dolorosa.

OLIVER. Stations of the Cross.

GABRIELLA. And underneath whitewash, pictures of our saints of orthodox religion.

    A little along, she is revealing heads of saints.

    Pretty bloody dull, I think.

OLIVER. So this place was orthodox before?

GABRIELLA. When we are Hungary, it Catholic, when we are holy Slavic people, Orthodox. When we have our friendly Turkish visitor who drop by for few hundred years, for while is mosque. When Napoleon pass through, is house for horses.

OLIVER. Stable.

GABRIELLA. Stable, yes. Clip clop.

OLIVER. But presumably it's built –

GABRIELLA. At turn of thirteen century. So can you guess now why I bring you here?

    Pause. OLIVER *looks at his watch.*

OLIVER. Now, look. Look, really, Mrs – Pesh –

GABRIELLA. Is 'Pecs'. Okeydoke. I tell you. Pronto.

OLIVER (*as a statement of fact*). I am in your hands.

During the following, GABRIELLA *takes bricks out of a different section of the wall.*

GABRIELLA. Now in 1989 we have great turnaround.

OLIVER. Agreed.

GABRIELLA. And everything is opened up. Including naturally files of secret police.

Slight pause. OLIVER *waves her on.*

And most of it is – recent, time of communists. But as secret police is very systematic in our country, files go way way back. For several hundred years. Some even in old Nagolitic language, before it become capital offence to speak it.

OLIVER (*to speed* GABRIELLA *along*). And so?

GABRIELLA. And so, cops pass on files to us at National Museum. And then guess what, I find in 1425, when we are vassal state of Ottomans, report of trial of so-called Italian merchant, Leonello Vegni, who come here from Padua and is tried as spy of Holy Roman Empire, found guilty and deheaded.

OLIVER. Or indeed '*be*headed'.

GABRIELLA. Or beheaded, yes.

OLIVER. And this report is in Old Nagolitic?

GABRIELLA. No I should coco. I tell you, capital offence, nobody speak it after thirteen hundred. Though it is interesting to note, since turnaround, some old words creeping back –

OLIVER *looks pointedly at his watch.*

GABRIELLA. But point is, in summary of trial, in nice new Slavic language, they explain how Signor Vegni's way of spying is to pose as connoisseur and report back to his master on all grand sight he sees. But actually, of course, he is really connoisseur, as well as really spy, and mixes truth and false. So it is hard to tell if when he writes he see 'octagonal basilica with fresco of our Holy Mother with dead Christ' is actually code for barrack with brigade of horse or . . . just what it says.

OLIVER *looks at* GABRIELLA.

As he say: 'A painting so akin to nature you might think it real'. To be compared to glorious work of his own Giotto di Bondone, hitherto unequal in all world.

OLIVER. I see. And what makes you think it's not a troop of cavalry?

GABRIELLA. Smart question.

OLIVER. Speedy answer?

GABRIELLA. Sure, like billyo. Now it is no surprise I think to find our country has great national patriotic poem.

OLIVER. None at all.

GABRIELLA. And in fourth canto famous legend about traveller journeying to Persia, who arrive in little village twenty league from Zabocz. And traveller made captive – what in old Nagolitic called 'involuntary guest' – and he is threaten even that he will be quite beheaded. But when sword is raise he promise if he will be spared he give to village gift much greater than his life. And to prove he take up brush and paint on church wall painting of Christ's followers and Virgin mourning Christ so natural and real its figures seem to live and breathe. And so they say he keep his bargain and they let him go. And everyone is most content, except for wise old man who say – neighbours, I fear this painting prove great price for us, that it prophecy of many miseries which fate inflicts on us throughout all centuries, that every mother looks on Virgin with dead son will one day mourn their own.

OLIVER. And was he right?

GABRIELLA. Well. It always said that painting was in Valley of Seven Churches.

OLIVER. Which is where?

GABRIELLA. Which lie indeed bit near Zabocz.

OLIVER. And which –

GABRIELLA. And which is laid waste by Turks in 1392.

Slight pause.

OLIVER. But I take it you're persuaded that the painting was elsewhere.

GABRIELLA. You forgive please: 'take it'?

OLIVER. I – presume.

GABRIELLA. Old Nagolitic too has its peculiarities.

OLIVER. You stagger me.

GABRIELLA. Words for 'to' and 'from' are actually interchangable.

OLIVER. This would explain the taxis.

GABRIELLA. But only if cab driver speak Old Nagolitic.

OLIVER. Which has been a capital offence since – . . .

GABRIELLA. – blah-di-blah.

GABRIELLA *is clearly waiting for* OLIVER *to guess where she's going.*

OLIVER. In Hindi, as I understand it, the words for 'tomorrow' and 'yesterday' are the same.

GABRIELLA. Well, blow me down.

OLIVER *decides to catch up.*

OLIVER. And so . . . you are – presumably – persuaded that the painting in the poem might not have been laid waste by Turks, but could have been the Lamentation Vegni may have seen in fourteen blah-di-blah. And if it was, then it's just about conceivable – though hardly likely, surely – it could still exist. And if it might have been few kilometres *to* Zabocz instead of *from* – depending naturally where you started –

GABRIELLA. Bingo. And so, I go round churches in 20 kilometre – circle?

OLIVER. Radius.

Now she is handing bricks down again.

GABRIELLA. Of Zabocz. And I tell my friends I am – mending country cottage?

OLIVER. Well, 'repairing' . . .

GABRIELLA. Good, so I can borrow tools and I tap away on walls and scrub at whitewash and I chip away at plaster and I pull out brick . . . And it is some time but eventually I find – voilà.

GABRIELLA *has uncovered a section of whitewash, in the middle of which a rough oval has been cleaned away. In the oval is the face of the Virgin holding Christ's naked body, partially obscured by a solid-looking rock in the foreground. It is clear there is a good stab at perspective, a bent arm is foreshortened, and the Virgin's face betrays great emotion.*

I guess I go that way and I find St John.

She is climbing down.

I think – single point perspective. Kind of. Figures occupy real space. Foreshortening. Individualised emotion. So, in short –

GABRIELLA *is down. Pause.*

OLIVER. In short, your Italian knew his cipolle.

GABRIELLA. Forgive please?

OLIVER. Onions. In that it's very like a Giotto.

GABRIELLA. Yes.

OLIVER. But you're not suggesting that it is a Giotto.

GABRIELLA. No.

OLIVER. Completed on a hitherto undocumented Balkan holiday.

GABRIELLA. Ha ha.

OLIVER. But a kind of – copy. By a follower. Hm. Interesting.

GABRIELLA. Not exactly.

OLIVER. Not exactly interesting?

GABRIELLA. Not exactly – copy.

Slight pause.

OLIVER. Mrs Pecs, I'm sorry. But this does appear – thus far at least – to be, well, shall we say, akin, to Giotto's Lamentation in the Arena Chapel, Padua.

GABRIELLA. Yes.

OLIVER. So either it's by Giotto, or it's the most remarkable coincidence in the history of art, or it's a copy.

GABRIELLA. Copy? You think that this is copy?

OLIVER. Well, I'd need to see the rest of it.

GABRIELLA. But this is not possible.

OLIVER. I must assure you, it happens all the time.

GABRIELLA. Or only possible in Hindi. If tomorrow really yesterday.

Pause.

OLIVER. When was – your national patriotic – thing, composed?

GABRIELLA. In early portion of twelve hundreds.

OLIVER. Giotto started painting the Arena in 1305.

GABRIELLA. Or thereabout. I know.

She holds the ladder, as an invitation for OLIVER *to climb.*

You want close butchers now?

OLIVER. Mrs Pecs, why did you bring me here?

GABRIELLA. Because if I am right that painting with perspective even kind of painted before Giotto born, then I think I make pretty damn substantial finding here.

OLIVER. To put it mildly.

GABRIELLA. So naturally I want just little bit to know if it will be true. And if so how best I proceed.

She gestures at the ladder. OLIVER *climbs far enough to see the surface of the painting.*

OLIVER. What solvent did you use on this?

GABRIELLA (*proudly*). Hydrogen peroxide.

OLIVER. What?

GABRIELLA. My sister is hairdresser. Most effective.

OLIVER. So it would appear.

GABRIELLA. This is not good?

OLIVER turns from the painting.

OLIVER. And does – does your museum know about this?

GABRIELLA. No-one knows about this. Present company excluded.

OLIVER comes down the ladder.

OLIVER. Should you not tell them?

GABRIELLA. I tell you.

OLIVER. You see, I'm sure, that you have, in this country, many expert –

GABRIELLA. You know that's bullshit.

OLIVER. And really, honestly, it's not my field –

GABRIELLA. Forgive please? Senior Professor, Ruskin Institute?

OLIVER. Just senior fellow, I'm afraid. In the Department of Contemporary Art Theory. So, actually, you see –

GABRIELLA. Okeydoke. Alrighty. Leave it to our great·National Museum. After all, it is our painting. And we are responsible, grown-up democracy. And either it is hogwash and we are laughing stock or it right and we try to clean with hairdye and we are clumsy clods, destroying priceless work of art.

OLIVER. I didn't – for a moment –

GABRIELLA. You think we don't know what you say? East Europe. Where even crooks don't know what icons worth. Where you pick up masterpiece for string of beads. Where everything is ugly and pathetic. Where they botch up socialism and make even bigger botch of market system too.

OLIVER. Well, I must assure you, back at home –

GABRIELLA. And what we spend on meal for you is tip. And you can buy our whole machine tool industry for thirty second ad on NBC. And sure we have funny language and we all have names which sound like horse's feet and sexual disease.

Slight pause.

OLIVER. I'm sorry. I –

GABRIELLA. So *here*? We have great genius painting which change history of art? What, here? In such a country make such botch of everything it touch? Well, I should bloody coco.

Pause.

OLIVER. Yes.

Slight pause.

I'm sorry. It's just basic British insularity. It's suddenly the papers are all full of places one had always vaguely thought to be made up.

Slight pause.

If not Slovenia, then certainly Slavonia. And then suddenly

concentration camps start springing up all over pastoral Shakespearian locations.

GABRIELLA. And now I guess we drive back to your grand important meal presumably.

A car screeches to a halt outside. GABRIELLA *goes quickly to put out the spotlight.*

OLIVER. What's this?

GABRIELLA. Shh. Shh.

OLIVER (*whispers*). The police?

GABRIELLA (*whispers*). Perhaps. Or . . . we are very near main autoroute.

OLIVER. Which means –

The door of the church is opened. A mid-teenage GIRL *enters with a middle-aged* SWEDISH MAN. *They don't see* GABRIELLA *or* OLIVER, *who move back into shadow.*

GIRL (*speaking in the language of our country*). Tova e myastoto. Bezopasno e, nikoy ne idva took. [This is the place. It's safe, nobody comes here.]

The GIRL *goes and gathers up the curtaining, to fold it over as a makeshift mattress.*

SWEDISH MAN. Do you have English?

GIRL. Ne. [No.]

SWEDISH MAN (*in German*). Oder Deutsch? [Or German?]

GIRL (*German*). Ein bisschen. [Little bit.]

SWEDISH MAN. Wir machen es hier? [We do it here?]

GIRL. Richtig. [That's right.]

The GIRL *has made the 'bed'.*

OLIVER (*whispers*). What's happening?

GABRIELLA (*whispers*). What d'you think?

GIRL. Es ist zwanzig Mark. [It's 20 deutschmark.]

SWEDISH MAN (*opening his wallet*). Ich habe Krone. Es ist so egal wie Deutschmark. [I have Swedish krona. It's as good as Deutschmark.]

GIRL. Nein. Es muss Deutschmark sein. [No. It must be Deutschmark.]

SWEDISH MAN. Dollars?

GIRL. Ja. Fünf Dollars ist gut. [Yes, five dollars is OK.]

She waits for the SWEDISH MAN *to hand over the dollar bill, but he folds the note and puts it in his own outside pocket for payment later. The* GIRL *shrugs and lies down on her back.*

OLIVER (*whispers*). He's German?

GABRIELLA (*whispers*). Swedish I think.

SWEDISH MAN. Um – Darf ich von hinten? [Um – can I have it from the back?]

GABRIELLA (*whispers*). He wants it from behind.

GIRL. Es ist mir gleich. [All right by me.]

GABRIELLA (*whispers*). She doesn't mind.

The GIRL *goes on all fours.*

SWEDISH MAN. Verstehst? Ich will Arsch ficken. [You understand – I want anal sex.]

GABRIELLA (*whispers*). Does she understand, he is wanting anal sex.

GIRL. Es ist mir gleich. [It doesn't matter]

GABRIELLA (*whispers*). She doesn't mind.

The MAN *kneels behind the* GIRL.

SWEDISH MAN. Ich habe kein Gummi. [I don't have a condom.]

GABRIELLA (*whispers*). He doesn't have protective.

GIRL. Es ist OK. [It's OK.]

GABRIELLA (*whispers*). She doesn't mind.

The MAN *is pulling up the* GIRL's *skirt when* OLIVER *speaks loud enough for him to hear.*

OLIVER. St John the Who?

The MAN *and the* GIRL *freeze.*

GABRIELLA. Forgive please.

OLIVER. You said, the Church was dedicated to St John someone. St John who?

GABRIELLA. Originally, St John Climacus. Catholics call it after St John Evangelist. I don't know what they call when mosque.

The MAN *stands, and runs out. The* GIRL *jumps up, but she's missed him.*

OLIVER. Please – forgive?

We hear the car door slam and see the arc of the headlamps as it turns and drives away. The GIRL *turns to* OLIVER *and* GABRIELLA:

GIRL. Cocksuckers.

She marches furiously out. Pause.

GABRIELLA. Why do you ask?

Slight pause.

OLIVER. Because we still don't know for sure this was the Lamentation Vegni saw. And one way to nail it would be if his letter named the church.

GABRIELLA. But we don't have letter. Just report in trial.

OLIVER. In which case, it's a fair bet that he sent it. And it presumably arrived.

Slight pause.

GABRIELLA. So then, you'll help me?

OLIVER. Yes.

GABRIELLA. Well. Blimey.

OLIVER looks at his watch.

OLIVER. That is, as long as –

GABRIELLA. Yes. of course.

She is going to put the bricks back.

May I ask why?

OLIVER looks at the scrumpled curtaining on the floor.

OLIVER. Because . . . because . . . This is Illyria, lady.

Lights fade.

Scene Two

Scaffolding has been erected in front of the painting. There is a platform at the bottom of the painting itself, about six feet above the ground, and a ladder going up and down. Bricks have been removed, most of the plaster and some of the whitewash. So we can sense the outline of the Lamentation. Also on the platform there are cleaning materials and boxes of electronic equipment, some of them opened. At ground level there are more boxes, a computer console (the computer is on and flashing), a telephone (with modem) and a nearly empty noticeboard.

At ground level, there are two PRIESTS: the Orthodox, middle-aged and bearded Father Sergei BOJOVIC and the younger Catholic Father Petr KAROLYI. They have brief cases and – as do most people – their car radios. There is also a SOLDIER near the computer console, with an automatic weapon. A SECOND SOLDIER stands 'guarding' the equipment.

GABRIELLA sits on the platform, her feet dangling over the edge. OLIVER, who is standing, moves to take a close look at a section of the painting. The SOLDIER notices.

FIRST SOLDIER (*waving his gun at* OLIVER). Ay!

Furious, OLIVER *goes to* GABRIELLA.

OLIVER. Vandalism.

GABRIELLA. Well, I tell you.

OLIVER. But *vandalism.*

The SECOND SOLDIER, *bored, looks inside one of the open boxes.*

GABRIELLA. I tell you. It just what they say.

OLIVER. It's what I've been accused of.

GABRIELLA. It – it just way they say in legal code. You know, like if you are dissident they call you 'hooligan' or 'parasite'.

OLIVER. I thought all that had changed.

GABRIELLA *shrugs as* OLIVER *notices the* SECOND SOLDIER.

OLIVER (*to the* SECOND SOLDIER). Excuse me. *Excuse* me.

The SECOND SOLDIER *looks questioningly at* GABRIELLA, *who gestures that he should leave the equipment alone. He does, with a contemptuous shrug.* OLIVER, *gesturing at the* PRIESTS:

OLIVER. And who the hell are they?

Slight pause.

GABRIELLA. Well, one with beard obviously East Rite Church. What you say Orthodox. One with clean shave usually Catholic.

OLIVER. Well, let no-one say you're spiritually stuck for choice.

GABRIELLA. Oh not so much choice. Basically, historical and geographic. It all depend, who is most long in charge.

OLIVER. You mean, which party?

GABRIELLA. No, which country. In south, where maybe people bit more backward, longest under Turk. And Turk bit happier with Orthodox. In north, for more time more Hungarian, and so more people Catholic, and naturally most civilised and up-to-date. Which all persist up to our present day.

OLIVER *has seen the* FIRST SOLDIER, *on ground level, playing with the computer.*

OLIVER. Indeed. Please forgive me, for a moment.

OLIVER *shins down the ladder.*

I wonder, could you stop that, please?

The FIRST SOLDIER *carries on tapping at the keyboard.*

FIRST SOLDIER. I think –

OLIVER. This is actually not your property.

FIRST SOLDIER. I think – you have message.

OLIVER. Just – don't touch.

FIRST SOLDIER. You have message, via modem.

OLIVER. Please. Just leave it.

The SOLDIER *does, shrugging.* OLIVER *tries to switch the computer off, but fails. The* FIRST SOLDIER, *automatically, moves in to help.*

OLIVER. *Leave* it.

The FIRST SOLDIER *shrugs again.* OLIVER *looks up to* GABRIELLA, *who pats the platform next to her, to request him to return. Breathing deeply,* OLIVER *climbs up and joins* GABRIELLA *once more.*

OLIVER. Speaking of hooligans.

Slight pause. OLIVER *looks at his watch.*

And it is half past ten. And the Minister was due at nine.

GABRIELLA. I notice, you always glancing at your watch. Do you never throw caution to four winds and take it off?

OLIVER *looks balefully at* GABRIELLA.

OLIVER. Perhaps, faced with the prospect of our project being – aquisitioned by the Pastorate of St Goliathos the Sensitive, and despite my naturally notorious sang-froid, stiff-upper arse and consequent tight lip, I am unable quite to emulate your enviably icy Balkan calm.

Slight pause.

Also this is not the first time I have been stood up by your Minister.

GABRIELLA. And in this you not so much unique. Put mildly.

OLIVER *looks at her.*

GABRIELLA. Hey. My arse it not so stiff. I do not want our fresco kissed and rubbed and bashed about with bells and smeared with candle grease. But I learn in time that anger finite quantity one should not squander needlessly. And softly softly often best way catch your monkey.

OLIVER (*mollified*). To coin a phrase.

Slight pause.

So where do you fit in?

GABRIELLA. To what?

OLIVER. To the great historical divide.

GABRIELLA. Oh, I think is pretty childish by and large. I do not pay these matters much attention. I am European.

OLIVER. Isn't everyone?

An impressive car slam causes everyone to look towards the door. A middle-aged man in a black leather coat enters, carrying a car radio. The man – whose name is PUSBAS *– turns to* KAROLYI.

PUSBAS *(in the language of our country)*. Pristigna li ministurut? [Has the Minister arrived?]

KAROLYI *(glancing at his watch)*. Oshte ne. [Not yet.]

PUSBAS *sees* BOJOVIC, *marches over to him, gesturing towards* OLIVER.

PUSBAS. Tova li e groopata razboynitsi? [This is the group of vandals?]

BOJOVIC. Khorata na izkoostvoto, da. Ministurut pristigna. [The art people, yes. The Minister is coming.]

PUSBAS. Choodo e, che sa gi poosnali dotook. [It's a mystery they've been allowed in here.]

OLIVER. Is that the Minister?

GABRIELLA. No fear. That is group called 'Nasledstvo'. They march about and dig up body of people killed in period of negative phenomena and think everything is plot of international masonry.

OLIVER. Nas – ledso?

GABRIELLA. 'Stvo'. I guess you will say 'Heritage'.

Enter Mikhail CZABA, *the Minister. He is in his late 20s, dressed in fashionably baggy clothes, and carries a car radio. He is followed by his dazzlingly beautiful female* SECRETARY *into the centre of the church.*

CZABA *(seeing the assemblage of people, to himself)*. Well, holy shit.

GABRIELLA. Now that is Minister.

OLIVER. Well, blimey.

CZABA *(in our country's language)*. E, gospoda, kakvo e tova? [Well, gentlemen, what's this?]

BOJOVIC, KAROLYI *and* PUSBAS *move in on* CZABA, *gesturing with their car radios, and speaking more or less simultaneously. The* SOLDIERS *smarten up,* OLIVER *and* GABRIELLA *stand.*

BOJOVIC. Uvazhaemi gospodin ministur, vizhdate kakvo stava. Tozi chovek oonishtozhava tsurkvata. [Esteemed Minister. You can see what's happening. This man is destroying the church.]

Overlapping with:

KAROLYI. Iskut za sobstvenost na pravoslavnata tsurkva e yavno nevaliden. [The claim by the Orthodox church to ownership is obviously false.]

Overlapping with:

PUSBAS. Nie ot Nasledstvo nastoyavame tezi choozhdentsi da budut izgoneni! [We in Tradition demand that these foreigners be expelled!]

CZABA. Ta znachi tova e rabotata? [And this is the work being done up here?]

CZABA *hands his radio to his* SECRETARY – *who puts it in her shoulder bag – and starts to climb the ladder up on to the platform.*

BOJOVIC. Te veche oonishtozhikha beztsenno izkoostvoto s dookhovno stoinost. [They have already destroyed an artwork of great spiritual value.]

KAROLYI. Me interesoova dali sudut e oovedomen i, kakvo vie predlagate da se napravi po vuprosa. [My concern is whether or not the courts have been informed and what action you propose to take.]

PUSBAS. Koi e naredil tezi khorata da budut dopoosnati took? Po chiya zapoved sa vneseni tezi su'orozheniya? [On whose instructions have these people been allowed here? On what authority was this equipment imported?]

CZABA *has reached* OLIVER *and* GABRIELLA *on the platform.*

CZABA. Dobro ootro, kazvam se Mikhail Czaba. [Good morning, I am Mikhail Czaba.]

GABRIELLA. Kazvam se Gabriella Pecs. [They call me Gabriella Pecs.] And this is Dr Oliver Davenport, of Ruskin Institute in London.

CZABA. Dobur den. [Good day to you.] (*English, with American inflection.*) Hi there I'm glad –

PUSBAS (*interrupts*). Gospodin ministur, nastoyavam da popitate tozi chovek – [Mr Minister, I must insist you ask this man –]

CZABA (*raising his finger*). Now, out of courtesy to our distinguished guest, does anyone have problem that we speak in English?

PUSBAS. I certainly have problem.

CZABA. Surely not.

PUSBAS. In principle.

CZABA. But clearly not in practice. So, we can all be good Europeans, speaking in American. Now, listen up. I'm running kind of late, so we have ten minutes only I'm afraid. Professor Davenport, you must forgive me, since three weeks ago I am supposed to be at dinner with you. Sadly, our currency is choosing that night to make bungee-jump, and I am otherwise engaged. My name is Czaba, I am Minister for Conservation of the National Monuments.

OLIVER. I thought that it was 'restoration'.

CZABA (*he tries the our country word*). 'Zapazvane'. Too close to call.

OLIVER. Depending I suppose on what you thought of what had happened to your national culture recently.

CZABA. Well, yes, sure. But our difficulty as I understand that in our country we have now law of Restitution, intending to return all property expropriated by state since 1940 to its rightful owner.

BOJOVIC. Which depend I must say naturally which state.

CZABA. So maybe you see problem.

BOJOVIC. As I must say for example this church is built in national faith.

KAROLYI. But its most recent use of course is Catholic.

CZABA. It is same with factories and country homes.

BOJOVIC. It is more recent Catholic because in 1940 Roman Church in thrall to aristocratic-military regime who are themselve in thrall to Nazis. Hence Catholic Bishop hands it to SS for special centre.

PUSBAS. I have to state that Iron Legion is in thrall to noone.

CZABA. Sad to say.

KAROLYI. In fact, of course, as Father Bojovic is well aware, it was not handed over but expropriated. For three weeks. Whereas for the last 40 years, as the whole world knows, the Orthodox obedience has demonstrated amply why it is so called.

BOJOVIC. I must say this easier to say from London than from here.

CZABA. Now, guys . . .

KAROLYI. All of which has little bearing on Professor Davenport's discovery, which is in fact we gather now agreed to be a work completed in the early 13th Century –

BOJOVIC. In fact is not agreed at all.

KAROLYI. – by an itinerant Italian on a journey east –

BOJOVIC. Or equally by unknown national artist of a late Byzantine time –

KAROLYI. – and in considerable advance of other paintings of its period –

BOJOVIC. – with element of earlier Italian style.

PUSBAS. Oh of course if it is national artist then it must be copy.

BOJOVIC. In fact I do not think I say –

PUSBAS. Or if advance it must be foreigner.

OLIVER. Whereas, in fact, whatever may turn out to be its history, this painting is not my 'discovery'. I am here purely in an advisory capacity, assisting Mrs Pecs, who is Deputy Chief Curator of the Early Modern section of the national Museum.

BOJOVIC. Acting Deputy Chief Curator, I must say.

OLIVER. Who through a quite remarkable combination of detection, application and frankly vision, has discovered a piece of work in the Giottan manner that may prove – to put it no more dramatically – to be of considerable interest to art historians.

Slight pause.

So if acting, acting pretty bloody well.

CZABA. I'm sorry – Gottan?

OLIVER. Giottan. As in Giotto.

CZABA looks blank.

OLIVER. The Trecento – 14th century – Italian master.

CZABA. And you reckon this thing painted earlier than 14 century?

OLIVER. It is still a matter of dispute.

CZABA. Well, holy – smoke.

OLIVER. But if I am asked my opinion about the future of the building . . .

CZABA. Please.

OLIVER. I would say it should revert to its most recent function. As a secular museum.

BOJOVIC. I think most recently it dump.

OLIVER. In which Mrs Pecs' potentially priceless find can be properly conserved, and studied, and appreciated.

KAROLYI. Mr Czaba, as is surely obvious to everyone –

OLIVER. Or at least that's what I thought till I became aware of the extent of passion in this case.

PUSBAS. What's this?

GABRIELLA waves at OLIVER in alarm.

OLIVER. For certainly our sponsors would be most unhappy to be seen to be infringing anybody's legal rights. Particularly religious rights. To a degree which might well threaten their involvement.

Slight pause.

Our Italian, and – German sponsors.

Pause.

CZABA. Professor Davenport, what say we take five here.

CZABA to the head of the ladder.

BOJOVIC. In privacy?

CZABA. That's right.

He invites KAROLYI, BOJOVIC, PUSBAS *to ascend, and* OLIVER *to descend*:

Maybe during we are gone Mrs Pecs may tell you all about this painting. And bring you up to speed on why and whether it is painted when and where. Oh, and naturally by whom.

Now CZABA, OLIVER *and the* SECRETARY *are at ground level, with* KAROLYI, BOJOVIC, PUSBAS *and* GABRIELLA *above.*

CZABA. Babel's Stairway.

OLIVER. Sorry?

CZABA. Is it not Babel, where God invent all different language, to stop mankind build stairway to heaven?

OLIVER. I think it's, in fact it's Babel's Tower.

CZABA. Of course. I am thinking of Led Zeppelin.

OLIVER *doesn't get this but acknowledges anyway.*

OLIVER. Now, look-

CZABA. And now maybe we cut crap and come clean with our bottom line here.

OLIVER. Sorry?

CZABA. I mean, it obvious what our black-suited comrades want. They want they own building with priceless painting on wall. You too, I guess.

OLIVER. I – just want to find the truth.

CZABA. Sure. Me also. And as great Lenin teaches, often best way to find out truth to ask whose interests are served.

OLIVER. I'm surprised you learn from Lenin.

CZABA. But of course. But with opposite effect. To me, to serve your interest is good. And frankly dear Professor I see through I think this flim-flam about 'considerable interest'. In fact I think that if this painting will be what you say, you find great hot-shit art discovery?

Slight pause.

OLIVER. In fact it's – not Professor. Merely Doctor.

CZABA. Well not so merely I dare say.

OLIVER. But yes. You're right. If the fresco predates Giotto then it could be viewed as the starting point of 600 years of western art.

CZABA. And it found by you and Mrs Pecs. And you clean it and you put up light and you unveil it at grand ceremony and you write big book and you go round campuses with talk and you go down in history as people who make biggest art find since King Tut or maybe even digging up Pompeii. And this for love of Mike not in your interest?

OLIVER. It isn't – *merely* in my interest.

CZABA. Oh sure. Interest also of truth beauty and universal European values.

Slight pause.

Listen. I know. You pick it up I don't know who your great painter is. You think – this man who has not heard of great Italian master, he is Minister of Culture, whatever fancy name they use. And you recall those past days – maybe you are visitor – and you lecture on your work at our great University and you think how nice it is that everybody speak good English and know so much more about your subject than your students back at home. And you go on peanut-costing tram and you see pretty girls with nice dress and nice hair and they are reading Tolstoy or Turgenev and you think in England they are dressed like tramp and reading garbage pail. And of course it's sad you come back and you find – yes, when they have choice, Turgenev goes in trashcan and instead it's video of Star Trek if not Terminator Two. And sure, I take your point. But I tell you, Doctor, it is price worth paying.

OLIVER. Really?

CZABA. Oh you bet your sweet boots Dr Davenport.

Slight pause.

This shocks you?

OLIVER. No.

CZABA. Fess up.

OLIVER. No, truly. As it happens, I've never seen a firm distinction between art and artefact. I certainly don't think a work's devalued if it operates within a market. I think that Star Trek works, for what it is, as well as Pride and Prejudice. Or even that up there.

CZABA. Well, whop that thing.

OLIVER. It's just that that was done – may have been done – the best part of a hundred years before we thought it was. Which is why it is in both our interests – as well as of our sponsors and your Ministry of Tourism – not to mention naturally your foreign currency reserves – if it is removed from here and remounted in your National Museum.

CZABA. Removed?

OLIVER. That's right.

CZABA. You can do that?

OLIVER. Sure. You stick a canvas and gauze facing on it, soaked in rabbit skin glue, let it dry, and yank it off. They used to do it all the time.

CZABA. They used to?

OLIVER. It's become, like many things, somewhat unfashionable among the current, minimalist tendency of fine art restoration. I'm sorry, conservation. But however out of favour, it would mean one set of clergy gets the church, your national museum gets the painting, and you get the biggest tourist trap since the Chinese terracotta army. So everybody's happy. Even Lenin.

CZABA. How long do you need?

OLIVER. A month?

CZABA. I give it my best shot.

As he turns to go back up the ladder, CZABA *notices the flashing message on the computer.*

I think that you have message.

As OLIVER *turns to the screen, he catches the* FIRST SOLDIER's *eye.* CZABA *is climbing the ladder.*

OLIVER. Um . . .

CZABA. I guess you access it and then you print it. It's like fax, only it come straight on to your hard disk.

He nods to the SECRETARY, *to come to* OLIVER's *aid. She moves in.*

SECRETARY. Excuse me?

OLIVER. Thank you, yes.

The SECRETARY *is not sure about the first step on the keyboard.*

FIRST SOLDIER. Mislya, che tryabva da vlezete v 'action menu'. [I think you need to get into the Action Menu.]

SECRETARY. Yasno. [Right.]

By this time, CZABA *has arrived on the platform:*

KAROLYI. E, Ministre? [Well, Minister?]

CZABA. Gospoda, izvinyavam se, gospozho i gospoda. Sama sudut mozhe da reshi vuprosa za sobstvenostta na sgradata. Mislya, che tryabva da pozvolim na doktor Davenport da produlzhi sledstvieto moo. [Gentlemen, I'm sorry, lady and gentlemen. Only the courts can decide about the ownership of the building. I think we must allow Dr Davenport to continue his investigation.]

BOJOVIC. Oovazhaemi gospodin ministur, oomolyavam vi da prerazgledate reshenieto si. [Esteemed Minister, I must beg you to reconsider.]

KAROLYI. Tova e bezobrazie! Az protestiram nai-kategorichno! [This is outrageous! I must protest in the strongest terms!]

PUSBAS. Predooprezhdavam vi, che moyata organizatsiya nyama de se ogranichi samo s protesti! [I must tell you, there will be more than mere protests from my organisation!]

As soon as the above is established:

SECRETARY. OK.

OLIVER. Is – can you get it?

The printer bursts into life.

SECRETARY. Is grass green?

OLIVER. Well done.

They go to the printer, OLIVER *once again catching the* SOLDIER*'s eye.*

SECRETARY. In fact, I am not so too much use to IBM compatible.

OLIVER. It's supposed to be – state of the art.

OLIVER *joins her watching the fearsomely fast printout. Above,* CZABA *continues his pitch.*

CZABA. Razberete, che sum s vurzani rutse. Neshtata ostavat vuv vlastta na sudut. [You must understand my hands are tied. The matter rests with the court.]

BOJOVIC. Ami ako ima oshte shteti? [But what if there is further damage?

CZABA. Az opredeleno smyatam, che sgradata e v sigurni rutse. A sega tryabva da vurvya. [I really think the building is in safe hands. Now, really, I must go.]

CZABA *goes to descend the ladder, followed by* BOJOVIC, KAROLYI, PUSBAS, *and* GABRIELLA.

SECRETARY. Hot money is on AppleMac to clean up east of Oder.

She tears off the message, and hands it to OLIVER.

OLIVER. Is that so.

CZABA *arrives in the workstation area.*

CZABA. Dr Davenport. You get your message?

OLIVER. Yes . . .

With a preoccupied nod to the SECRETARY.

Yes, thank you very much . . .

CZABA *(filling in)*. All Ministers get drop dead gorgeous secretaries. But mine has wordprocessing and one hundred word per minute shorthand also. So no surprise I am envy of whole cabinet.

Most of the PRIESTS *have arrived*:

I have told our friends that you have our permission to continue with your investigation, pending final ruling by our court. On understanding naturally there is no substantial alteration to building's fabric.

OLIVER (*quietly*). The paint layer is a millimetre thick.

CZABA (*quietly*). Well, you don't say.

Louder, to cover:

You know, I have theory that big problem with high culture is it makes you think too much of past. You go to opera, see painting, all time they are reminding you of dreadful precedent, how everything goes wrong before. Which is why if you want real change, you put barbarians in charge. People who don't know about how walls will all fall down. Who don't know history of Tower of Babel.

OLIVER *looks quizzical.* CZABA *drops his voice again*:

CZABA. I'd say, you have two weeks.

CZABA *turns and goes, followed by his* SECRETARY.

PUSBAS (*to* OLIVER). Don't worry. We'll be back.

PUSBAS *and* KAROLYI *go out. The* FIRST SOLDIER *gestures to the* SECOND. *The* SECOND SOLDIER *leaves, but the* FIRST *decides to wait by the church door.*

BOJOVIC. Dear Dr Davenport, there is something you must understand about this country. It will always prove last barrier. To Russia from above, to Muslim from below. As has always been, way back into Byzantine days. You stand on Europe's battlement. Take care.

BOJOVIC *turns and goes towards the church door. As he reaches it, the* FIRST SOLDIER *buttonholes him, gesturing back to* OLIVER. *and they go out together, the* FIRST SOLDIER *talking. Meanwhile*:

GABRIELLA. Well? *Well?*

OLIVER. What does 'Climacus' mean?

GABRIELLA. Forgive please?

OLIVER. As in St John. The patron of this church.

GABRIELLA. What, literally?

OLIVER. Literally.

GABRIELLA. It mean ladder. St John is monk who writes most famous book called Ladder of Divine Ascent. Each chapter is called – what is this thing?

OLIVER. Rung.

Slight pause. BOJOVIC *and the* SOLDIER *have gone.*

GABRIELLA. It come you see from Greek word for 'ladder'. Which in fact is Klimax.

Slight pause.

Which of course in English means 'Big Finish'. And has sex meaning too I think.

OLIVER. Yes. Yes, it does.

He looks at the letter. GABRIELLA *looks inquiringly at* OLIVER.

And you were right. Softly softly did catch monkey. He will let us take it down.

GABRIELLA. What, take off wall?

OLIVER. That's right. And remount it in the national musuem.

GABRIELLA. And this is good?

OLIVER. Well, only if we're right.

GABRIELLA *realises the significance of the printout in* OLIVER'*s hand.*

GABRIELLA. And are we?

Pause.

OLIVER. Well, they did find the letter. It was in an archive that had not been opened since the death of Emperor Maximilian the First. And there was indeed a description of the painting, which was quite detailed, and included both a foreground rock and the fact that St John's right arm was outstretched towards the Virgin, as if perhaps to comfort her. And while Vegni doesn't make any direct comparison with Giotto's Lamentation, he does note the similarity between the painter and 'our great Italian masters of last century'. Which is as he himself points out all the more remarkable, in view of the painting being mentioned – celebrated, even – in a noted national epic poem composed no later than 1220.

Slight pause.

Oh, and he names the church. It's San Giovanni della Scala. 'Scala' means 'ladder', in Italian.

He starts to climb the ladder to the platform.

So it looks like, you were wrong. You didn't botch it. You have great genius painting after all. The starting pistol for the next 600 years. Here of all places. The frontier between the mediaeval and the modern world.

He reaches the platform and looks down at GABRIELLA.

Mrs Pecs, it seems you've made the biggest art find since the un-earthing of Pompeii. What say we take a butchers at the rest of it?

Scene Three

Two weeks later. On the platform, RESTORERS *in white dungarees are preparing the painting for removal from the wall. This involves painting a layer of glue on sections of the painting and then affixing 40 by 40cm pieces of loose cotton gauze – themselves steeped in glue – on the surface, stretched out gently by hand. This procedure starts from the bottom of the painting and moves upwards. As they work, the* RESTORERS *are listening to music on walkmans.*

The workstation area below has also developed. There are some new creature comforts: an armchair, a coffee machine. There are also microscopic machines now unpacked and in operation, and a big noticeboard on which a black-and-white, sectioned photograph of the painting is displayed, along with other lists and data, and repro-ductions of other Lamentations (including Giotto's at Padua). The computer is on and the screen is presently showing an outline of a section of the painting.

Suddenly the door opens and LEO KATZ, *an American in his 30s, marches in followed by two* SOLDIERS. LEO *has come straight from the airport with his luggage and duty free bag. The* SOLDIERS *do not need to be same as in the last scene. The* FIRST SOLDIER *is smoking.*

FIRST SOLDIER. Ne, ne. Not passport. Propoosk. Pass.

LEO. Look, I don't have a pass.

The FIRST SOLDIER *looks at the* SECOND SOLDIER.

FIRST SOLDIER (*to the* SECOND SOLDIER). No pass.

LEO. You see, I've come straight from the airport.

FIRST SOLDIER. Eh?

LEO. I use the word 'straight' loosely.

FIRST SOLDIER. So you want go airport?

LEO. Never again.

FIRST SOLDIER. No pass, no entry.

LEO. Hey. Is Dr Davenport around?

The FIRST SOLDIER *looks at the* SECOND SOLDIER, *who stands.*

SECOND SOLDIER. Dr Davenport not here. He is come back at twelve o'clock.

LEO. Well, hey, that's my appointment.

SECOND SOLDIER. What?

LEO. Twelve o'clock. He is come back to see me.

The SOLDIERS *look at each other.*

It is ten of already. Can I not wait?

The SOLDIERS *look at each other. the* FIRST SOLDIER *decides to angle for a bribe.*

FIRST SOLDIER. Duty free.

LEO. That's right.

FIRST SOLDIER. Jack Daniels.

LEO. Correct.

FIRST SOLDIER. And cigarette?

LEO. No, I don't smoke.

He picks up his bags.

And no more should you.

As he carries his bags over to the workstation area.

It is a fucking house of worship, for Christ's sake.

The SOLDIERS *decide it's too much trouble to make an issue of this.*

FIRST SOLDIER (*in the language of our country*). Abe, kazval li e anglichaninut, che ima sreshta s nyakovo? [Did the Englishman say someone was coming to see him?]

SECOND SOLDIER. Ne. No toi yavno govori istinata. [No. But he is obviously right.]

FIRST SOLDIER. Da, znam. Mean bastard!

LEO, who knows exactly what he is doing, smiles to himself as he puts down his bags. He notes that the work on the painting is going on above him. He looks round the workstation area, noting the telephone. He takes a letter from his pocket and goes and picks up the phone. He tries to make sense of it.

LEO. Now is this a busy or a dial tone.

Slight pause.

Hallo?

OLIVER and GABRIELLA enter the church. GABRIELLA has her car radio. The FIRST SOLDIER is about to tell OLIVER about his visitor, but decides against it, as the conversation is in full flow. OLIVER and GABRIELLA are getting on well with the task in hand and each other, and are in an excellent mood.

OLIVER. No, my contention is not that national stereotypes are true, but that if they aren't true they aren't true in spades.

LEO puts the telephone down, and quickly moves his luggage somewhere inconspicuous.

GABRIELLA. Forgive please? Spades?

OLIVER. To the opposite extreme. So there is nothing *less* efficient than an inefficient German. No-one *less* frugal than a spendthrift Scot.

LEO *goes up the ladder.*

GABRIELLA. Nothing less miserable than cheery Russian.

OLIVER. Right. And no-one more engaging than an interesting Belgian. No-one ruder than a discourteous Japanese.

LEO *looks at the painting and the work going on. He is noticed after a moment by a female* RESTORER. GABRIELLA *puts down her car radio.*

GABRIELLA. Nothing meaner maybe than ungenerous American.

OLIVER. Your experience has clearly been quite different from mine.

OLIVER *and* GABRIELLA *are taking their overcoats and jackets off, and changing into white coats.* LEO *is looking closely at the painting as yet uncovered.*

RESTORER. Dobur den. Good morning.

LEO. Morning.

OLIVER. Nothing quieter than a restrained Italian.

RESTORER. Can I help you?

LEO. No, I'm fine.

OLIVER. Nothing more prosaic than an unromantic Pole.

LEO. Just carry on as if I wasn't here.

GABRIELLA. And English?

The RESTORER *returns to her work.*

OLIVER. What do you think?

GABRIELLA. Nothing as – loose-lipped –

OLIVER. Or indeed loose-arsed . . . as an –

GABRIELLA *touches his lips with her finger, just a moment longer than is necessary for the demonstration:*

GABRIELLA. It is impossibility to conceive.

A moment between them.

OLIVER. I am told that the South Ibo word for – 'arse', is in North Ibo the first person pronoun singular.

Slight pause.

GABRIELLA. Big deal.Old Nagolitic word for – ladies' place, new language word for 'flute'.

OLIVER. Leading no doubt to all kinds of droll misunderstandings in the orchestra.

LEO *is descending the ladder.*

LEO. I am reliably informed by people paid to know these things that the Finnish word for 'fart' is the Swedish for 'speed'.

OLIVER *and* GABRIELLA *look at each other and the new arrival.*

LEO . As of course the British for 'apartment' is the American for 'puncture'.

GABRIELLA. You forgive please?

LEO. Flat.

OLIVER. Uh, may I ask –

LEO. Pretty neat set-up you got up there. You're going for a strappo?

OLIVER. Stacco.

LEO. No kidding. Coletta or a resin?

OLIVER. Um – coletta.

LEO. So you reckon it's all painted wet?

OLIVER. Uh –

LEO (*to* GABRIELLA). Coletta's a water-based adhesive. It dissolves medium – paint – applied to a dry surface.

OLIVER. Yes, Mrs Pecs knows that. And no, it's mostly but not all buon fresco. So we're using polyvinal acetate to fix the secco.

Now LEO'*s going to the computer.*

LEO. State of the art. Now this is Getty software, right?

OLIVER. Now, look, are you a journalist?

LEO. Kind of. Now how d'you get the palette on this thing?

OLIVER *takes over. He is now more adept at using this machine and gets a print-out almost immediately:*

OLIVER. I'm told it's more or less what you'd expect. Lime white, red and yellow ochre, burnt sienna, ultramarine –

LEO. You're told?

OLIVER. By people paid to know these things.

LEO (*to* GABRIELLA). And the reflectography and photogrammetry and all that stuff checked out?

GABRIELLA. Yes, thank you. Hunkydorily.

LEO. But you're basically dating on the provenance? Some . . . poem.

OLIVER *leaves the computer. He wishes he knew* LEO'*s game.* LEO *himself takes the print-out of the palette and pockets it.*

GABRIELLA. Our great national poem. Which is composed at latest by twelve hundred twenty-five.

LEO. That early. Boy.

OLIVER. No earlier than Magna Carta.

LEO. But I'm right, to date the thing that soon, you need to to tack the poem to, some letter, from some envoy?

OLIVER. Spy.

LEO. Hey, I bet you guys are praying that you got it right.

Pause.

OLIVER. What do you mean?

LEO. Because without the poem, it's a copy of the Giotto Lamentation in the Arena Chapel, Padua.

LEO takes a postcard of the Padua Lamentation from his pocket and hands it to OLIVER. He goes to the photograph of our painting and points out the differences.

I mean, one arm is headed forward, and the old girl's turned into a rock, and instead of angels you got stars . . . But all the kind of errors you'd commit if you were drawing from a drawing. Or from memory.

OLIVER. There is no problem with the provenance.

LEO. Well, fingers crossed. But, hey. It's always scary, wanting anything so badly to be true.

Pause.

OLIVER. Who are you?

LEO. Oh, I'm sorry.

He makes a bit of a meal of searching for his card in his wallet.

OLIVER. I am H.O. Davenport.

LEO. That's Dr, Senior Fellow, Ruskin Institute.

OLIVER. And this is Mrs Gabriella Pecs, of the National Museum.

LEO (*handing his card to* GABRIELLA). Ah, and you're the folks who get the fresco, right?

GABRIELLA. How do you do?

LEO. Oh, hunkydorily.

GABRIELLA hands the card to OLIVER.

But I do need a phone.

He is already there and using it. OLIVER *has read the card and closes his eyes.*

GABRIELLA. You dial eight and then number.

LEO. *Eight.*

He dials, taking the number from the letter.

OLIVER. You're Leonard Katz.

LEO. But my chums all call me Leo.

Down phone:

Hi, this is Professor Katz.

OLIVER. Well, let's not rush to judgement.

LEO. English?

Slight pause.

Hey, is that 27612? It's Professor Katz from Cornell University.

GABRIELLA. What is he?

OLIVER. He's an art historian.

GABRIELLA. Not journalist?

OLIVER. In the sense that Pol Pot was an urban redeveloper.

LEO*'s got the right person on the telephone.*

LEO. Ah, hi. Yuh, sure, no problem. Took the pretty way.

GABRIELLA. So he is presumably bad news?

OLIVER. Spot on.

LEO *suddenly asks* GABRIELLA:

LEO. Hey, when d'you pull?

GABRIELLA. When dry. Tomorrow.

OLIVER. Why d'you ask?

LEO (*down phone*). It's tomorrow so you'll have to shift. Move
quickly. Sure. Bye bye.

He puts the phone down.

OLIVER. Now, Profesor Katz, I have to make it plain –

LEO. Me too. Four points. First of all, to 'make it plain' that thus far I
have not had a good day. Due to some error of judgement, Mrs
Pecs, I flew your national airline, which is to civil aviation what
Van Gogh was to cosmetic surgery. Then, two, this may turn out to
be five points, at passport control the guy reads out my name –
which is Leonard Aaron Katz – and quips, 'Israeli passport, no?'

OLIVER *looks at* GABRIELLA, *who bites her lip.*

And we haven't even gotten *in* the taxi.

GABRIELLA (*to lighten the atmosphere*). In fact, in our old language,
'to' and 'from' are only distinguishable by context.

LEO. I beg your pardon?

GABRIELLA. This significant pecularity accounting maybe for some
shortcoming of taxicabs.

It hasn't worked.

LEO. Mrs Pecs, I know a little of your country's history. I am aware
for instance of your enviable record under German occupation.
Only 80,000 of your Jews deported to the camps in Poland. This
heartening statistic is accounted for however by the fact that by the
time the Germans got round to deporting them, there weren't that

many more than 80,000 left. So, three, I think it's probably unlikely
that we're going to get along.

OLIVER. Now, I naturally haven't asked, but I would guess that Mrs
Pecs is at the very outside 35 –

LEO. And it is no surprise to me, point four, that having found a
dubiously provenanced but interesting fresco all of two hours from
the airport even driving straight, you plan to rip it off its wall and
shove it into a collection whose major works consist of portraits of
the Mighty Leader pinning medals on Young Pioneers and blessing
tractors.

GABRIELLA. This is not true. We have Gentile Fabriano and young
Brueghel.

LEO. You have a copy of a school of Fabriano and your Brueghel is at
best a distant cousin. You should also know you've a section of St
Nicodemus' drapery as verdigris in secco which it obviously can't
be as it's fugitive and at a quick glance two protruding nails.

OLIVER. This is a travesty.

LEO. The nails? I must assure you, buddy –

OLIVER. Your description of our aims and purpose in this transfer.

LEO. Oh, which are?

OLIVER. Well, the main intention, obviously, is the protection of the
work from the considerable environmental risks –

LEO. What, 'to save the village it was necessary to destroy it'?

OLIVER. Sorry?

LEO. General Westmoreland in Vietnam.

GABRIELLA. What has this to do with Vietnam?

OLIVER. Smart question. You see, Gabriella, Professor Katz has
made something of a career of bowling round the world attacking
restoration beg their pardon conservation projects on the grounds
that Michelangelo took 500 years of candlegrease and overpainting
into full account when he did the Sistene ceiling, and thus actually
intended it should turn dark brown –

LEO. Now this *is* a travesty.

OLIVER. Whereas, in fact, for all this guff about 'acknowledging the
painting's history', what it comes down to for Professor Katz and
ilk is that they want their art – and more crucially their artists – to
be ancient, brooding and mysterious. So that we're rendered totally
dependent on the insight of historians to explain their tortured
genius to us. Whereas –

LEO. Whereas the problem with the scrapers, – Gabby, is that for all
their spritz about the artist's original intentions, they too have
prejudices, which is for things that look as bright and bland and

squeaky clean as television. And if as they believe there's no real difference between a quattrocento Venus and a pin-up, and the Sistene back wall's just a billboard, then why not strip 'em down and make 'em look that way?

GABRIELLA. But presumably no-one takes seriously this –

OLIVER. As opposed that is to the Professor, who does not see painters as the makers of material objects in the context of their place and time at all –

GABRIELLA. But decidedly it is not possible for serious art critic –

OLIVER. – but rather as essentially no more than tubes through which God pours unique and universal truths upon the world.

GABRIELLA. But this is surely actually true.

Pause. OLIVER is forced to turn to GABRIELLA.

OLIVER. Look. Look. I have no problem with the notion of good painters. I just don't think they're fundamentally diffcrent from other kinds of maker of other kinds of thing.

GABRIELLA. So presumably if Leonardo will be alive today, he directs advert for Pizza Hut?

LEO. That is exactly what he thinks.

OLIVER. That is a – grotesque parody of what I think.

GABRIELLA. I am pleased because that utter bullshit to my mind.

LEO *laughs.*

GABRIELLA. And if you have last 40 years as we have, you will see how it bullshit too.

Pause.

OLIVER. What do you mean?

GABRIELLA. I mean, during 40 years we are having no great artists and all social and historic context, and this means our museums full of children's crayon drawings and old quilts and bits of painted cart because naturally we must combat petit-bourgeois formalism and acknowledge art of heroic revolutionary masses quite as good as Michelangelo. So I tell you what I think. I think there is great painting and there is also less great and there is pretty bloody bad as well.

To LEO:

And I don't know if it come from God or love or what you have for breakfast. But if something great and beautiful defaced, and made ugly and pathetic, then we must scrape clean, and restore to what it was before.

LEO. But surely, you shouldn't wipe out all that history?

GABRIELLA. No? Whyever not?

LEO. 'Cos it'll be forgotten.

GABRIELLA. Maybe some things best forgotten.

OLIVER (*gently*). So there was no value in the last 40 years?

GABRIELLA. No. There was no value absolutely in last 40 years.

Father BOJOVIC *enters with a young* POLICEWOMAN *carrying a document case and a car radio.*

BOJOVIC. Professor Katz? I'm Father Bojovic.

LEO. Ah. How do you do.

BOJOVIC. I truly please to see you I must say.

LEO. I'm – pleased to be here.

BOJOVIC. And you will be meeting Dr Davenport and Mrs Pecs?

LEO. Yes, I surely have.

OLIVER. Forgive me, what is this?

LEO. Oh, did I not explain? I am here at the invitation of Father Bojovic. As an expert witness in the suit he's bringing to prevent the – the removal of this most intriguing artwork from this wall.

BOJOVIC. Suit which bring forward till tomorrow. I must say, in nick of time, it seem.

BOJOVIC *nods to the* POLICEWOMAN *who hands a document to* OLIVER.

BOJOVIC. This order for you to be at court. What I think you call subpoena.

OLIVER *looks at the document.*

It in our language I'm afraid.

OLIVER *hands the document to* GABRIELLA.

Also it forbidding naturally from you take artwork down.

LEO. Well, hey. The US Cavalry.

GABRIELLA *nods to confirm the content of the document.* OLIVER *breathes deeply.*

OLIVER. This is – too ridiculous for words. I will have to fax Milan. And Munich.

BOJOVIC *looks impassive.* OLIVER *glances at the computer. He decides against risking failure.*

Gabriella, can I take the car?

GABRIELLA *hands him the keys.*

GABRIELLA. I will check out all these nails and naturally remove them.

She goes up the ladder to join the RESTORERS. OLIVER *goes briskly out. The* POLICEWOMAN *gestures to* BOJOVIC *to go.*

BOJOVIC *gestures that he'd like to stay a little.*

BOJOVIC. So Professor, do you have good flight?

LEO. Oh, um, you know.

BOJOVIC. You fly Lufthansa, I assume?

LEO. No, not exactly.

BOJOVIC. Ah. And may I enquire, if you have time yet to form opinion?

LEO. What about the fresco?

BOJOVIC. Yes of course.

Slight pause.

LEO. Well, it's a hard shot. Their dating seems improbable, to say the least. But it could be right. It's tough to call.

Pause.

BOJOVIC. I must say, it is refreshing to hear scholar who confess he does not know.

LEO. Well, we've hardly anything to go on. Only one percent of Byzantine paintings have come down to us. So we're thrown back on the documents, which are themselves fragmentary, subject to misquotation, mistranslation, printing errors . . .

BOJOVIC. Ah, yes. Sometime I think I must say if this gift of writing is so wonderful. When Catholics come to liberate from Mongol yoke, they ban not books but language. It no surprise I think great national poetry and song – work which stretch out to embrace a people's soul – is pass on not by eye but ear. So it great comfort I must say that with all this –

Gesturing to the equipment.

– it is still hard shot to call.

LEO. I am naturally pleased to be a comfort.

BOJOVIC. On other hand . . . It in our interest, still, that you say 'no'.

Pause.

LEO. Father, that's how I earn my living.

BOJOVIC. Saying 'no'?

LEO. Saying to those who would abuse these fragile objects: 'let them be'.

BOJOVIC *smiles. The* POLICEWOMAN *is pointedly looking at her watch.*

BOJOVIC. But now our lift maybe is grown impatient.

LEO. Our lift?

BOJOVIC. The police kindly offer you quick run to Hyatt Regency.

LEO. Can't wait.

BOJOVIC (*to* POLICEWOMAN). Tryabva da si vurvim. [We must go.]

LEO *goes to pick up his bags. A thought strikes him.*

LEO. Um, father. Your great national poem.

BOJOVIC. Yes?

LEO. It was orally transmitted? Mouth to ear?

BOJOVIC. Of course. Indeed, it is not poem really, more national song. It is sung to gusle, our great national instrument, by mediaeval troubadour.

LEO. I see.

BOJOVIC *turns to go.*

LEO. So when was it first written down?

Scene Four

The next day. Outside, it is pouring with rain. The canvas and gauze facing of the painting has been completed. Anna JEDLIKOVA, who is 50 and soberly dressed, stands on the platform looking at the now concealed painting, slightly bemused. In the workstation area below, Father KAROLYI stands with his umbrella looking at the photograph of the painting. After a moment, JEDLIKOVA shrugs and starts to climb down the ladder. KAROLYI recognises her.

KAROLYI (*in our country's language*). Tova ne e li Anna Jedlikova? [It is not, Anna Jedlikova?]

JEDLIKOVA. Ami, da, tya e. Sreshtali li sme? [Well, yes, it is. Have we met?]

KAROLYI. Ne, no se radvam da se zapoznaem. Kazvam se Petr Karolyi. [No, but I'm pleased to do so. My name's Petr Karolyi]

He puts his hand out.

JEDLIKOVA. Proshtavaite, da ne bi da ste sinut na Tomaz Karolyi? [I'm sorry, not the son of Tomaz Karolyi?]

KAROLYI. Da. [Yes.]

JEDLIKOVA. Kakva neochakvana sreshta. [Well, how unexpected.] Well, father, maybe we should speak in your adopted language.

Slight pause.

KAROLYI. At home in London we spoke our mother tongue.

JEDLIKOVA. Since you return no doubt you hear great change.

KAROLYI. Well, yes-

JEDLIKOVA. We shake off language of international working class and take on speech of middle ages.

> KAROLYI *smiles uncertainly.*

KAROLYI. Is this so bad?

JEDLIKOVA. Well, I am not so sure we fight since all these years to stop our neighbours share our word for postage stamp or petrol station or umbrella.

> KAROLYI *shrugs.*

> So I am happy with all chances to brush up my English. Now I may use it for more thing than 'do you hear news from Moscow' and 'careful here come guard'.

KAROLYI. I'm sorry?

JEDLIKOVA. Having learnt it not in harsh English school but delightful second category camp in Bejec.

> KAROLYI *gets it.*

KAROLYI. In fact, it's not so harsh.

JEDLIKOVA. Oh no? I thought in English system it is sitting dumb in rows and if you speak they hit your bottom with long stick.

KAROLYI. No. this is by no means accurate. In fact, it is well understood today, that children may do anything they like, as long as they are wearing the right shoes.

JEDLIKOVA. While in Bejec this is hardly option.

KAROLYI. No.

> *Pause.* KAROLYI *decides not to pick up on* JEDLIKOVA's *tone.*

> In fact, my only problem is my father changed his name from Karolyi to Karol. Unfortunately no-one tells us 'Carol' is a girl's name. A little trying, for a young boy in an English school.

JEDLIKOVA. Oh, well. To change your name is surely price of exile. Didn't Trotsky take his jailor's?

> LEO *enters, shaking the rain from his coat.* KAROLYI *decides he can't ignore* JEDLIKOVA's *acid tone.*

KAROLYI. So it is true.

JEDLIKOVA. What's true?

KAROLYI. You do resent us.

JEDLIKOVA. Who?

KAROLYI. The people who got out.

JEDLIKOVA. You are then no more than twelve years old I guess.

KAROLYI. Well, then, my father?

Slight pause.

JEDLIKOVA. Well, maybe.

Pause.

KAROLYI. It is a little harsh, perhaps. In a society which, as everyone accepts, offered the choice of being hangman, victim or accomplice. To say: you cannot choose to get out if you get the chance.

JEDLIKOVA. Except of course there are some people who do not accept such choice. And pay the price. As your father knows full well.

KAROLYI *shrugs and turns to go.* LEO *is about to make himself known to* JEDLIKOVA. *But then she collars* KAROLYI.

JEDLIKOVA. OK. I tell you what I think. You leave, you stop to be a witness. Worst story that I ever hear, in second world war, Serb children are transport to camp at Jasenovac, and they are so hungry that they eat cardboard tags around their neck. Which is their family, their age, their name. They eat their history. They die, and nobody remember them.

Slight pause.

And now, already, here, our past is being erased. And exiles with new names come back, and restore old names of streets and squares and towns. But in fact you cannot wipe it all away, like a cosmetic. Because for 40 years it is not normal here. And so we must remember. We must not eat our names. Otherwise, like Trotsky, we might end up with our jailor's.

JEDLIKOVA *turns to* LEO.

Yes?

LEO. Your honour? My name's Leo Katz. I'm an – expert witness.

JEDLIKOVA. Ah. How do you do.

They shake hands.

KAROLYI. Your honour?

JEDLIKOVA. Oh, forgive me. I presume you know. For my sins, I am presiding magistrate.

KAROLYI *didn't know.*

JEDLIKOVA. Yes. I am jailor now.

OLIVER *and* GABRIELLA *hurry in,* GABRIELLA *pumping the rain off her umbrella.*

GABRIELLA (*to* JEDLIKOVA). Izvinyavaite, dvizhenieto po aootostrada beshe uzhasno. [I am so sorry, the traffic on the autoroute is terrible.]

JEDLIKOVA. Molya vi. Na men mi beshe priyatno da ostana za malko sama. [Please, I was happy to have a moment or two on my own.]

To OLIVER:

I'm afraid some thing do not yet change. Black Cosmo passes, and all traffic light go green. So where is Father Bojovic?

OLIVER. He was – I think we overtook him on the motorway.

GABRIELLA. In his 1980 Laika.

KAROLYI, JEDLIKOVA *and* KAROLYI *all know the significance of this.*

JEDLIKOVA (*to* OLIVER). Hey. Perhaps you don't know difference between Laika and Jehovah's Witness?

OLIVER. No.

JEDLIKOVA. You can shut door on Jehovah's Witness.

LEO. You have Jehovah's Witnesses already?

Slight pause.

JEDLIKOVA. Oh, yes. And we have also Sunday Coming people, glamour contests, ice-dispensers. All mod cons. I think we wait five minutes. Then we must begin.

JEDLIKOVA *withdraws to set out chairs in a rough semicircle. GABRIELLA, OLIVER, LEO and KAROLYI are left uncomfortably together. After a pause:*

OLIVER. How's the hotel?

LEO. It's fine. The clientele consists almost entirely of Americans with names that end with yitch and yuck who have come back to reclaim estates their grandfathers abandoned 40 years ago.

GABRIELLA. I think not so much abandoned.

LEO. One guy from Michigan is now proud owner of the paediatric wing of the International Friendship Hospital. The plan is for a hot-shot nite-spot, with showgirls drawn exclusively from the Olympics women gymnast's team.

GABRIELLA. This to coin phrase is grotesque parody.

LEO. And tell me, does it bother anyone that as the opera houses close, the synagogues are being desecrated? That Vietnamese and gypsies – and Ukrainians – are beaten up by skinheads on the streets and everyone applauds? That as the walls fall in the west, there's new ones rising just as high the other side?

Slight pause.

I mean, I merely ask.

GABRIELLA. Oh yes. You 'merely' ask. Well, I should bloody coco.

She is very angry.

You have – you know that you have no idea. You have – actually – no idea.

LEO *and* OLIVER *are a little taken aback.* GABRIELLA *moves to stalk away, then turns back.*

GABRIELLA. And in answer to mere question, no. I don't see just because of war, we have to be trashcan for world misfits. Or Ellis Island for all huddled masses en route to wild west. OK, so bad things happen. Very bad. But that is since 50 years ago now actually. Why should we be world transit camp? Why should we get rid of Russian army and get Russian dregs and scum in place? To coin phrase, in spades?

OLIVER. So, um, a huddled mass is a heroic mass without a visa?

GABRIELLA. Oh, ha bloody ha.

Slight pause.

No, actually, it poem carve on Statue of Liberty New York. 'Give me your huddled masses, wanting to breathe free'.

LEO. It's 'yearning'. 'Yearning to breathe free'.

GABRIELLA. Well, tallyho.

Now she does stride off to the side. KAROLYI *smiles dryly and goes to look at the photographs on the noticeboard. Pause.*

LEO. Um, is she always –

OLIVER. No.

Pause.

LEO. So, um, is there a Mr Pecs?

OLIVER. No longer.

LEO (*'That explains it'*). Ah.

OLIVER *looks dangerously at* LEO *as a dripping Father* BOJOVIC *enters.*

JEDLIKOVA. Ah. Father Bojovic.

BOJOVIC. Oovazhaema gospozho sudya. Kolata mi se schoopi. Zakusukh na aootostrada – [Esteemed madam magistrate. My car broke down. I was stranded on the autoroute –]

JEDLIKOVA. It is no matter. Now maybe we begin. Please, everybody, take a pew.

EVERYONE *sits. As they do so,* OLIVER *hands* GABRIELLA *a document.*

OLIVER. Are you all right.

GABRIELLA. Just hunkydory, thank you.

OLIVER. Okeydoke.

JEDLIKOVA. Right now, gentlemen and lady. This afternoon is most informal. We are concerned entirely with request for taking down of painting. Our task today does not concern at all with ownership of building and I will not discuss that matter at this time. And in support of international understanding, we will all speak English.

BOJOVIC. Respected magistrate, I must object.

JEDLIKOVA. Already?

KAROLYI *gestures to* BOJOVIC *not to push this at this stage.*

BOJOVIC. Very well. Withdrawn.

LEO *looks a little quizzical.* JEDLIKOVA *picks this up.*

JEDLIKOVA. Our western guests will please forgive us. But we are all infants in this business. Of real trials with real outcomes.

Pause. She opens a file.

Now, Dr Davenport. You drag us all out here so we appreciate full situation, and I must say I am mildly disappointed to find painting is wrapped up in bandage.

OLIVER. Well, it can all be readily explained.

JEDLIKOVA. Well, please proceed.

OLIVER. By Mrs Pecs, the Director of the project.

JEDLIKOVA *and* OTHERS *had expected* OLIVER *to lead off.* OLIVER *gives* GABRIELLA *a good luck wink. She is working from the notes prepared with and handed to her by* OLIVER; *she is nervous but determined.*

GABRIELLA. Um – Respected magistrate. We drag you here today for two   three reasons. First to show how this procedure to transfer painting – which you may hear accused to be a yanking off or ripping off or skinning off or flaying – is actually technique developed in middle ages and used to great effect for all time since.

She looks at LEO, *challengingly.*

JEDLIKOVA. Professor Katz?

LEO. Yes?

JEDLIKOVA. Do you wish to comment on this at all?

LEO. No. No, this is all fine.

Slight pause.

JEDLIKOVA (*to* GABRIELLA). Please carry on.

GABRIELLA. However, we also want show you *reason* for transferral. For though painting has survive so many century of candle-grease and sprinkling of holy water, shaking cause by bells –

KAROLYI. Well, it is a religious painting.

GABRIELLA. What may be it cannot endure so well is to end up half way from zinc smelting works to major international autoroute. Particularly as painting faces back on autoroute and has one layer of brick remove.

KAROLYI. By you.

OLIVER. Yes of course by us.

BOJOVIC. And not just layer of brick I ought to stress.

JEDLIKOVA. Yes, yes. Professor Katz, this is all OK with you?

LEO. Oh, sure. Just hunkydory.

Slight pause. GABRIELLA *is alarmed by* LEO's *silence but decides to plough gamely on.*

GABRIELLA. So, question obviously remain as to why this painting matter. It unheard of. Anonymous. As you see from photo, not in excellent condition. But there is quite enough to tell that very similar to fresco of Italian master Giotto, painted in thirteen hundred five. With main difference that lady from behind is rock, and St John instead of throwing arm back in gesture of despair, leans one arm forward as if to comfort Virgin in her grief. And this is naturally all kind of error you must make if you are drawing from a drawing, or else out of memory.

LEO *recognises the quotation from his own remark.*

GABRIELLA. Except. Except we think that it is not this look like Giotto but that Giotto look like this. And if we are right, then it – fountainhead of next 600 years. To coin phrase, starting shot of great race to change Europe out from state of childish mediaeval superstition into modern rational universal man.

Slight pause.

And you know such progress can seem less big deal, if you go through your renaissance and enlightenment, if you have your Michelangelo and Mozart and Voltaire. Maybe if you reach to journey's end then it bit more easy to say, actually, this being grown up maybe not so hunkydory after all. But, for us, it is maybe bit different. For us, being child not so far back. For those who stand on Europe's battlements since all of last 600 years.

Pause.

And yes it probably was painted here by foreigner. But maybe too you understand what it is meaning to us if despite all Turkish occupation, despite Mongol yoke, still this painting made, and wanted, asked for, and appreciated here. Maybe then we may feel bit more universal, bit more grown up, maybe even bit more European.

Pause. There is a moment between OLIVER *and* GABRIELLA. *Then she sits.*

JEDLIKOVA. Well. Thank you. Now –

BOJOVIC. Respected magistrate, to my opinion all of this is most instructive, but I must say not of relevance to question of removing painting at this time.

KAROLYI. Absolutely. There is surely no necessary connection between the painting's age and where it's ultimately housed. For otherwise –

LEO. Oh, but there is.

They turn to LEO. Pause.

JEDLIKOVA. Aha. Professor Katz.

LEO. For three – for several reasons.

JEDLIKOVA gestures to LEO to proceed. He in turn gestures to the computer equipment.

LEO. First being, you can understand how all these folks might get kinda jumpy, spending all this cash on evidence that frankly wouldn't stand up in a court of law in No Hope Idaho.

OLIVER. There is nothing suspect with the provenance.

LEO. Oh no? The letter of a spy, reporting home in code?

OLIVER. All Vegni's letter does is to confirm the National –

LEO. – the National Patriotic Poem.

OLIVER. Yes.

LEO. AKA Great National Patriotic Song.

OLIVER. Indeed.

LEO. Remind me. Which edition did you use?

Pause.

OLIVER. I'm sorry. Which *edition*?

LEO. Or rather, which transcription?

OLIVER. Which *transcription*?

OLIVER turns to GABRIELLA, who remains looking steadfastly away. BOJOVIC looks smug.

LEO. OK. Let's run this through. The thing is apparently first actually written down, by monks, in 1350. Intriguingly, not in the language of its composition, the use of which becomes a capital offence in twelve hundred eighty-five. So what we have here, people, is a plan to stick – not wrap – but stick a canvas bandage on the painting, hammer it all over with a rubber mallet, then force metal bars around the edges and then lever all or some of it away –

OLIVER. This is absurd –

LEO. – that's what they haven't scrubbed off yet with bleach –

OLIVER looks bleakly at GABRIELLA, who chooses not to look back.

LEO. – On the basis of the absolute reliability of a transcription and translation of a memorially reported song, as to the existence and description of a work of art completed, what? a hundred fifty years before? And with oodles of respect, it seems to me around conceivable that a mediaeval monk can embellish the description of a painting, with reference to one he may have seen himself. Shortly after it had been so ably copied, from the Italian original, in the charming church of St John Something, Cholovar.

Pause.

OLIVER. It is – I suppose, a possible interpretation –

LEO. *Possible*?

OLIVER. It hardly proves –

LEO. Spot on. What *proves* it, Olly, is right here.

He takes the pallette print-out from his pocket.

OLIVER. What's this?

LEO. Ultramarine? In, what, 1195?

Pause.

JEDLIKOVA. Would someone please explain?

LEO. Ultramarine is powdered lapis lazuli, a semi-precious stone found only in what's now north-east Afghanistan. It has very high infra-red reflectance, so on Dr Davenport's machine it shows up nearly white, on what's left of the Virgin's robe, St Nicodemus' mantle and the sky. And the general opinion is against its use in mediaeval Europe before at the earliest the middle of the 13th century.

Pause.

OLIVER. Look. Yes. But, look. It still, it doesn't absolutely –

LEO. No. Not absolutely, sure. But let's put it at its mildest. If you're trying to revolutionise the history of western art, it doesn't help.

Pause.

GABRIELLA. Is this right?

Slight pause.

OLIVER. I'm sorry. I did tell you. Not my field.

Slight pause.

Oh *damn*.

Pause.

JEDLIKOVA. So do I understand that painting is no longer what you say?

OLIVER. It seems – less likely.

JEDLIKOVA. And so then, presumably –

LEO. And so then, sure, presumably, Deutschelectronic and Peruzzi fold their tents and steal away. But before they go, your honour, I think it's worth enquiring why they came.

Pause. OLIVER *rises.*

OLIVER. What do you mean?

LEO *shrugs, smiling.*

LEO. Hey, come on, Olly. You know what I mean.

Slight pause.

OLIVER. No, I'm afraid I don't.

JEDLIKOVA. And nor do I.

Attention is back on LEO. OLIVER *sits. Affecting reluctance,* LEO *continues*:

LEO. OK. It's simple. What this operation does is to make the painting mobile. And sure, right now, it's only booked in for one trip. But does anybody really reckon that'd be the end of it?

LEO *gestures round the equipment.*

You really think, Peruzzi and Deutschelectronic, after all of this, would transport you to the National Museum, assist you with the heavy lifting, and then slope off home?

GABRIELLA *did.*

Come on. It'd be – hey, we got the big bang here, you can't keep it to yourself, what say we take it on a little tour? Just think of all that currency. Or rather, while you guys are sorting out security, maybe more like an extended loan? Or even, now we come to think of it, wouldn't it be actually much happier, and much more accessible to doctors and professors and their ilk, in a nice new hi-tech California gallery with state-of-the-art air conditioning and three gold trowels from Architecture Quarterly? Hey, come on, Olly, wasn't that the deal?

GABRIELLA *is appalled.*

OLIVER. This is – this is an absolute –

LEO. 'Cos that's what happens, Gabriella. That's what paintings are. They're stars, of the Hollywood variety. With tours. And fans. And franchised merchandise. And – entourage. And as such, they are, they must be, universal and eternal. Not allowed to change. Most surely, not allowed to fade. To crumble, or grow old. And of course, they'll never die.

Slight pause.

But paintings do grow old. Their history is written on their faces, just like it is on ours. And like the history of people, or of peoples, either you acknowlege it, and try to understand it, or you say it never happened, nothing's changed, and you end up doing it again.

LEO *looks directly at* JEDLIKOVA.

Hey, do you know, there were names here on the wall, from when it was a torture chamber, which they scraped away?

JEDLIKOVA *stands.*

JEDLIKOVA. I see no reason to delay my ruling. This procedure must now cease. The painting must remain, here in church. This facing can be taken off?

LEO. Sure. It comes off with water. And a little tender loving care.

JEDLIKOVA. Then please, Dr Davenport and Mrs Pecs, remove it.

She gathers up her papers and goes quickly out. GABRIELLA, furious and upset, throws down her notes and climbs the ladder to the platform. KAROLYI goes quickly to LEO.

KAROLYI. Well done Professor.

LEO. Well. Well, I –

KAROLYI *senses the approaching* BOJOVIC, *smiles, turns and goes.* OLIVER *follows* GABRIELLA *up the ladder.* BOJOVIC *to* LEO.

BOJOVIC. We have saying that best doctor is one who leave you no closer to your deathbed than before.

LEO. We have a saying, too. If it ain't broke, don't fix it. Please forgive me for a moment.

BOJOVIC. Naturally.

LEO *climbs the ladder. On the platform,* GABRIELLA *stands, apart from* OLIVER *still angry.*

LEO. Well, I told you, people. Wanting it so much.

GABRIELLA (*turns to* LEO). You shit. You cocksucker.

LEO. Hey now, chill out –

GABRIELLA. I say you have no idea. But it is me. I have no idea of how few you scumbags really comprehend.

LEO. Now loosen up here –

GABRIELLA. No, not me. You listen up. You know why this church turn to torture chamber? Because when Nazi come all Catholic are out in street with little flags waving like billyo, because now they get their hands on Jewish businesses and stores.

LEO. Hey. I have absolutely no relationship –

GABRIELLA. No, no, of course. You are brought here by our great national church. Which is indeed call Orthodox for no bad reason looking at last 40 years. And you say that being Jew is pretty bad in 1941-45. You bet. But is not too hunkydory actually since 1948 put mildly. And that is not to mention Mr Pusbas and his bald boys who think all this basically part of international Zionist conspiracy.

She looks defiantly at LEO.

And these people on your side. And up your arse. You cocksucker.

She jabs LEO *in the chest and turns away.* OLIVER *goes to her and puts his arm on hers.* GABRIELLA *flings it aside.*

GABRIELLA. No no.

OLIVER *turns to* LEO.

LEO. To coin a phrase. This is a travesty.

OLIVER (*indicating that* LEO *should leave*). But nonetheless, perhaps it's best, if you –

GABRIELLA (*turns to* OLIVER). And you.

OLIVER. I'm sorry?

GABRIELLA. Perhaps it best 'if you' as well.

OLIVER. What's this?

GABRIELLA (*heavily sarcastic*). I mean, must you not call up chums in Munich and Milan? And explain how you fail to get your mitts on big star painting? How you miss to clinch your deal?

OLIVER. Now that, that was –

GABRIELLA. Oh, yes. Big travesty. *I trusted you.*

Slight pause.

OLIVER. And you were right –

GABRIELLA. And I am thinking during all these days how everybody judge our painting. How for Catholic is spread of European culture, for national church expression of our holy Slavic soul. And for great Western intellectuals is either not so quite good photograph or megaphone of God. But even I do not think actually is international currency.

OLIVER. No more do I.

GABRIELLA. Whereas for me I must say painting very simple. It is like our poem beg its pardon song explain. How our country through all history will be betrayed. By occupying oh so sorry by protecting power. By our own High Priest and screaming mob. By seeming friend. And now by you.

She looks defiantly at OLIVER *and* LEO, *who gestures at the painting.*

LEO. OK. Let's cut the crap. You want to know what this is actually about?

OLIVER. Um, Leo –

LEO. 'Cos I frankly couldn't give a shit how old this is, who got what first and least of all how much it's worth.

A moment, then:

GABRIELLA (*defiantly*). Yes please?

LEO. 'Cos what *I* see's a guy who tells a story of a man who's actually a God who's put to death before his mother like a common criminal. And although he's heard it told a thousand times, he brings to it that innocence, that freshness and that rage we all feel when we hear a story first time round.

We begin to hear the approach of a noisy diesel engine through the speech.

Which I appreciate may not go down a storm round here. Where you had a chance to make the world anew, you built a prison camp.

The screech of a lorry braking, the slam of a door. BOJOVIC's *head turns towards it.*

And now the walls are down, you shut out all the other voices in the world – in all their rich variety – you throw up the portcullis and you sell yourself to fucking Disneyland. So, don't you –

The church door flies open. A long-haired Azeri with a metal leg enters, turns back, and calls:

RAIF (*speaking in Russian*). OK. Zdyes padaidyot. [OK. This will do.]

RAIF *is followed in by a Mozambican student and a middle-aged gypsy man. They are called* ANTONIO *and* NICO. ANTONIO *has an automatic weapon.*

GABRIELLA (*our country*). Ay-bogoo. Kakvo stava? [My God, what's happening?]

OLIVER. What's this – ?

LEO. Hey. Christ.

BOJOVIC. Kakvo e tova? [What is this?]

RAIF (*speaking in Russian, to* BOJOVIC). Atyets, miy ishchem oobezhishche. [Father. We wish sanctuary.]

BOJOVIC *sees that* RAIF, ANTONIO *and* NICO *are being quickly followed in by a motley group of* REFUGEES, *all of whom are dripping wet from the storm. They are an armed Afghan,* ABDUL, *who holds a gagged Englishman* DEREK, *a Palestinian woman,* YASMIN, *who is pushing in a young English woman* TONI – *also gagged and bound – followed by the middle-aged Bosnian* AMIRA, *who carries her cello in its case, a middle-aged Russian,* MARINA, *a young Kurdish woman,* FATIMA, *a young Sri Lankan woman,* TUNU, *a 30-something Russian called* GRIGORI, *and a teenage gyspy girl,* CLEOPATRA, *who pushes a pram. Many of the* REFUGEES *carry luggage, equipment, provisions and tools of various kinds, including two big cans of petrol.*

BOJOVIC. Az . . . ne . . . ne. Tova ne e tsurkva. [I – No. No. This is not a church.]

BOJOVIC *is moving to the door.*

RAIF (*Russian*). Miy bezhentsiy. Miy trebooyem, shtobiy viy predastavili nam oobyezhishche. [We are refugees. We demand you give us sanctuary.]

BOJOVIC. Ne vi razbiram. [I'm sorry. I don't understand.]

LEO. What are they saying?

GABRIELLA. They're demanding sanctuary.

BOJOVIC. Samo posetitel. [Just a visitor.]

He has managed to get to the door, and slips out.

OLIVER. Sanctuary?

GABRIELLA. You know, asylum.

ANTONIO (*Russian, shouting after* BOJOVIC). Eta zhe tserkof, svolach! [Isn't this a church, you bastard!]

RAIF *has drawn a handgun.*

RAIF. Miy dolzhniy ostatsa zdyes. [Well, we must stay here!]

OLIVER. They have a gun.

RAIF (*Azeri, to* YASMIN). Burada galmalıyız yokh? [Shouldn't we stay here?]

YASMIN *shrugs.*

ABDUL (*Arabic, to* YASMIN). baddu yaᶜraf iza badna nibga hown. [He wants to know if we should stay.]

YASMIN (*Arabic*). shoo badna nsawi gheir heik? [What else are we to do?]

ANTONIO (*Russian, pointing at* OLIVER *and* GABRIELLA). A kak biyt setimi lyoodmi? [What about this people?]

KAROLYI *enters the church.*

KAROLYI (*our country*). Kakvo iskate? [What do you want?] What do you want?

ANTONIO (*Russian*). Oobyezhishche. [Refuge.]

GRIGORI. Asylum.

KAROLYI (*Russian*). Eta nye tserkof. [This is not a church.] This is not a church.

Ineffectively, to LEO, OLIVER *and* GABRIELLA.

Run! You must run!

As EVERYONE*'s attention turns to* OLIVER, LEO *and* GABRIELLA, DEREK *makes a dash for it and escapes with* KAROLYI.

RAIF (*Russian*). Da astanovitye zhe yivo! [Stop him!]

YASMIN (*Arabic*). ni'fil il-abwaab. Shoofoo iza feeh makhraj taani. [We shut the doors. See if there are other exits.]

ANTONIO (*pointing again at* OLIVER *and* GABRIELLA). A kak biyt setimi lyoodmi? [What about this people?]

RAIF (*Russian*). Zastav ikh slyezt. [Make them come down.]

The doors are closed and locked.

ABDUL (*Turkish*). Qapıyı qapattım. Girilmez. [I have closed the door. It cannot be entered.]

RAIF (*To* NICO, *in Russian*). Viykhadiy. [Exits.]

RAIF *and* NICO *go and look for other exits.*

ANTONIO (*Russian*). Ladno. Slyeztye. Postepyenno, slyezaitye. [OK. Come down. Come slowly down.]

OLIVER. What's this?

GABRIELLA. It kind of Russian. He say we must come down.

ANTONIO (*Russian*). Postepyenno! [Slowly!]

GABRIELLA. Slowly.

LEO. Fine by me.

As LEO, GABRIELLA *and* OLIVER *climb down,* RAIF *and* NICO *return.*

RAIF (*Russian*). Droogikh viykhodov nyetoo. [No other exits.]

ANTONIO (*Russian, to* RAIF). Miy zaderzhim etikh lyoodyei zalozhnikami? [Shall we hold these people as hostages?]

YASMIN (*to* ABDUL, *in Arabic*). 'ul-luh laazim niHtijiz an-nas haadool. [Tell him we should hold these people.]

OLIVER. What are they saying?

ABDUL (*Turkish, to* RAIF). Bunlar rehin oldukhlarını, diyerler gibi tutmalarını gerekhtiyini söylüyor. [She says they're hostages. We should hold them like the others.]

RAIF (*Azeri*). Yakhshı. [Good.] (*To* ANTONIO, *in Russian*). Zaderzhim. [We hold them.]

YASMIN (*Arabic*). Naᶜam. [Yes.]

RAIF (*Russian*). Miy zaderzhali etikh lyoodyei! Ani zalozhniki! Na kalyeni, na kalyeni! [We keep these people! They are hostages! On their knees, on their knees!]

OLIVER, LEO *and* GABRIELLA *are pushed over to join* TONI. *Equipment is being brought from the door into the body of the church.*

OLIVER (*to* TONI). Who are they?

TONI. Who knows. Asylum seekers. We were ambushed at the border.

LEO. We?

TONI (*with heavy irony*). Mercy convoy. Humanitarian relief.

LEO *sees the cans being moved.*

LEO. What the hell's that?

TONI. Petrol.

RAIF (*Russian, to* ANTONIO). Ta dvyer zaperta? [Is that door secure?]

ANTONIO (*Russian*). Da, zaperta. [Yes, it's secure.]

TONI. *One* be observant, *two* try to rest, *three* advise of medical needs.

LEO. Beg pardon?

TONI. I once went to the Middle East. They show this video. Three do's and don'ts if you get taken as a hostage.

LEO. Let's run through the 'don'ts'.

TONI. It's *one* don't argue, *three* don't draw attention to yourself – and two I can't remember –

LEO. Try.

YASMIN. Yes please. That would be very helpful.

The HOSTAGES *look round at* YASMIN. *Pause.*

Well, perhaps a little later. Now, do you have passport please?

OLIVER *finds a card:*

OLIVER. In the hotel. Please do have my card.

TONI. Mine's in the lorry.

GABRIELLA (*hands over her ID card*). ID.

LEO (*hands over as insouciantly as possible*). Passport.

YASMIN *reads* LEO's *passport.*

YASMIN. Well. Leonard. Aaron. Katz. What a distinctive name.

She looks at LEO. LEO *looks at her.* YASMIN *goes and pulls forward* ABDUL, RAIF, AMIRA *and* FATIMA.

But now you change clothes. So if anyone burst in, you are a little less distinctive.

The HOSTAGES *look blank.*

YASMIN. You give your clothes to these people. And then they give you theirs.

ABDUL (*Turkish*). Ne oluyor? [What's happening?]

RAIF (*Azeri, to* ABDUL). Elbise deyishtirmemizi gerekhiyor gaaliba. [I think she is saying we must change clothes.]

ANTONIO (*Russian*). Razdyevaityes pazhalsta. [Take off your clothes!]

To TONI.

Take clothes off please.

LEO. Don't 'one'.

The HOSTAGES *begin to undress.* ABDUL, RAIF *and* AMIRA *start to undress too.* TONI *is aware of the* MEN *looking at her.*

TONI. I spend five years trying to get out of doing this.

YASMIN. Now your names are Raif, and –

To ABDUL *in Arabic*:

– eysh ismak? [What's your name?]

ABDUL. Adbul.

YASMIN. Abdul, and –

AMIRA. Amira.

FATIMA. Fatima.

YASMIN. You are now – Azeri, Kurdish?

ABDUL (*Turkish*). Afghanee. [Afghan.]

Pointing to FATIMA:

hiyya kurdeeya [She is Kurdish.]

YASMIN. Afghan, Bosnian?

AMIRA *nods.*

And Kurd.

OLIVER *stops undressing.*

OLIVER. In fact – you should know, that I'm actually diabetic –

YASMIN *looks at* OLIVER.

YASMIN. In fact, you should know – you are a different people now.

FATIMA *goes upstage to change behind a blanket.* OLIVER, GABRIELLA, LEO *and* TONI *continue to undress. Their* CAPTORS *stand watching. A* LOUDSPEAKER *breaks in suddenly from outside as the lights fade to blackout.*

LOUDSPEAKER (*in the language of our country*). Politsiya! Govori politsiyata! Nie sme mnogo! Narushavate zakona! Khvuriete oruzhiata i izlezte, sega! Povtoryavam: Nie sme mnogo! Narushavate zakona! Khvuriete oruzhiata i izlezte, sega! . . . [Police! This is the police! We are present in large numbers! You are breaking the law! Put down any weapons and come out now! I repeat: We are present in large numbers! You are trespassing in this church! Put down any weapons and come out now! . . .]

End of Act One.

ACT TWO

To call nationalism 'atavistic' or to proclaim
an anti-nationalist crusade is like proclaiming
a crusade against hydrogen in water.
The point is not to overcome nationalism
but to understand it.

Neil Ascherson,
Independent on Sunday, 31 January 1993

The new Serbia should include the existing republic of Serbia, as well as Vojvodina, Kosovo, Bosnia-Hercegovina, Macedonia, Montenegro and the parts of Croatia where Serbs live. Croatia should consist of what you can see from the top of Zagreb Cathedral.

Vojslav Sesilj, Serbian leader, August 1991

People all over Eastern Europe are refusing to be governed by those who do not speak their language.

Norman Tebbit, Newsnight, 10 December 1991

In Ivo Andric's novel, *The Bridge over the Drina*, a nineteenth-century Muslim shopkeeper tries to explain God's creation of Bosnia. 'When Allah the Merciful and Compassionate created this world', he says, 'the earth was smooth and even as a finely engraved plate. That displeased the devil who envied man this gift of God. And while the earth was still just as it had come from God's hands, damp and soft as unbaked clay, he stole up and scratched the face of God's earth with his nails as much and as deeply as he could. Therefore, deep rivers and ravines were formed which divided one district from another and kept men apart. And Allah felt pity when he saw what the Accursed One had done, so he sent his angels to spread their wings above those places and men learnt from the angels of God how to build bridges, and therefore the greatest blessing is to build a bridge and the greatest sin to interfere with it . . . '

Quoted in the Independent on Sunday,
19 June 1994

I am not willing to risk the lives of German soldiers for countries whose names we cannot spell properly.

Volker Ruhe, German defence minister,
December 1992

ACT TWO

Scene Five

The afternoon of the following day. A routine has been established, and little clumps of REFUGEES *have established themselves and their possessions around the church. They have been eating packaged food taken from the van when they arrived.*

The HOSTAGES *are sitting together, their hands tied behind their backs, wearing their unfamiliar clothes.* OLIVER *is presently absent,* GABRIELLA *sits near* TONI; LEO *sits a little way apart.* FATIMA *is nursing* CLEOPATRA's *baby.* CLEOPATRA *is sitting near the* HOSTAGES *with a notebook, in which she makes the occasional note.*

A ladder has been set up to a window through which the REFUGEES *can monitor the approach to the church door. At present,* ANTONIO *is up the ladder, looking out. He calls down to* RAIF. YASMIN *is standing beside him.* GRIGORI *is nearby.*

RAIF (*Russian*). Tebye shto niboot vidna? [Can you see anything?]

ANTONIO (*Russian*). Nyet. Anee vsyo oobrali. [No. They've moved everything back.]

RAIF (*Russian*). Vubshche nichevo? [Nothing at all?]

ANTONIO (*Russian*). A da. Kriysha, pokhozhe bolshovovo groozovika. Na nyei taryelka. [Oh, yes. There's the top of what looks like a big van. It's got a dish on it.]

RAIF (*Russian*). Eto dalzhno biyt . . . satellite. [That must be a satellite.]

ANTONIO (*Russian*). Shto tiy dumayesh? Politsiya? [What, you think police?]

GRIGORI (*Russian*). Nyet, skuryaiye vsyevo. Say-N-N. [No, more likely CNN.]

YASMIN. What does he say?

ANTONIO *is descending.*

GRIGORI. He says they move everything back. He think he see TV van.

YASMIN. No police? No helicopters?

ANTONIO. Not that I can see.

GRIGORI. Quiet. Damn quiet. Too quiet.

YASMIN *looks questioningly at* GRIGORI.

GRIGORI (*explaining*). Cowboy. Red Indian.

YASMIN. Well, they have twenty minutes. Till our deadline.

> *She moves away: a little later* RAIF *will descend. Now* ABDUL *brings* OLIVER *in, clearly from some makeshift toiletry arrangement.* ABDUL *has the pistol and feels the need to pull the hand-tied* OLIVER *back to his place.*

OLIVER. All right. All right.

> ABDUL *'helps'* OLIVER *sit down, shrugs, and moves a little apart.*

GABRIELLA. How are facilities?

OLIVER (*slightly snappy*). Well, they've not *demonstrably* improved since lunchtime.

> GABRIELLA *calls.*

GABRIELLA. Maybe quite soon they send in insulin! Before you will become in coma!

> OLIVER *swallows.* ABDUL *and* RAIF *look round.*

LEO (*sarcastic*). Three. 'Don't draw attention to yourself'.

OLIVER (*angry*). Well, doesn't that depend on the alternative?

> *This spat has attracted* YASMIN's *and* ANTONIO's *attention as well.* LEO *smiles to himself, humourlessly.* GABRIELLA *covers.*

GABRIELLA. Which is that we make best of it we can. And Toni tell us how things bottom out when she take good butchers at her sophisticated but essentially empty life as nationally-famous Third Page Girl and concludes well sod this for a game of soldiers.

OLIVER. Sorry?

GABRIELLA. Which is that she plan to lengthen profile –

TONI. Broaden.

GABRIELLA. And record this disc which called –

TONI. Which I'm talked into calling Heavy Petting.

GABRIELLA. And which bomb.

> *To* OLIVER.

And 'bomb' I think is bad.

TONI. And 'bomb' is terrible.

GABRIELLA (*to* TONI). So not like 'go a bomb'.

TONI. Hey. No.

GABRIELLA. And then –

TONI. OK, and then I gets took up by this arsehole with a blow-wave who assures me if I keep my boobs in from henceforward – which is fine by *me* – I'm due some seriously basic repositioning. And so

I ends up and-the-first-prize-is-this-Satsasuma-Microwaveing on a gameshow called Fame Sex and Match.

GABRIELLA. Which also bomb?

TONI. As does Atlantic City and the caper movie. So he says, look, doll, had you ever thought of dedicating your talents to the needs of others, and I says no way I'm doing skinhead retards in Romania or kids on drips in Sarajevo 'cos I'm sorry but I'm just not good with children, dogs or blood. And *he* says you should read the papers and I ends up mascot of a mercy dash to somewhere unpronouncable and we're in a lay-by half way up a border queue when we're hijacked by the Munsters, forced at gunpoint through a railway tunnel – backwards – and the rest is fucking history.

She remembers where she is, bites her lip and crosses herself.

Oops.

OLIVER. I'm sorry, did you say 'Fame Sex and Match'?

TONI. That's right.

OLIVER. And this is or was a British television programme?

TONI. Sure. Kind of a – raunchy remix of Blind Date.

OLIVER. Blind Date?

TONI. Blind Date.

Slight pause.

The television show.

Slight pause.

GABRIELLA. You know, sometime it quite hard to believe you two coming from same country.

Pause. OLIVER *laughs.*

OLIVER. Two nations divided by a common language.

GABRIELLA. Please?

OLIVER. Conventionally attributed to Bernard Shaw. He said it about Americans and Brits but – I was thinking of Disraeli.

GABRIELLA. Who?

TONI. Benjamin Disraeli. 18-oh-something to 1881. British Conservative Prime Minister. Later first Earl of Beaconsfield. Author of Sybil the Two Nations. Yup?

OLIVER *looks at* TONI *in some surprise.*

America is named after the Italian explorer Amerigo Vespucci.Words not in Dr Samuel Johnson's famous dictionary include 'euphemism', 'irritable' and 'anus'. And there are more nude boobs in the National Gallery in Washington than in a year's supply of Playboy Magazine. So don't *you* give me a hard time.

Slight pause.

LEO. In fact, Dr Davenport is of the view –

OLIVER. In fact, Dr Davenport agrees. You can't cut high art off from the culture that surrounds it.

TONI. Well, there you go.

During this, YASMIN *and* ANTONIO *approach.*

OLIVER. And, sure, if the quintessence of renaissance man is Michelangelo and his Risen Christ emerging shamelessly stark bollock naked from the tomb, then maybe now, yuh, it's a gameshow or a caper movie or a Playboy centrefold.

YASMIN. Ah. Michelangelo and Playboy magazine. The great art critic taking solace in the triumphs of western civilisation.

OLIVER *doesn't reply.*

YASMIN. Are you all right?

OLIVER. For now.

YASMIN. And when do you get ill?

OLIVER. Well, this doesn't happen very often. But – as I remember – it's not much more than a day. I mean – I'm already starting – to be thirsty, and to – need to use the lavatory.

YASMIN. Your friends outside who know all this presumably. Don't seem to care too much about you.

OLIVER. They wouldn't need to, if I wasn't kept a prisoner here.

YASMIN. That too is easily resolved.

OLIVER. You think so?

YASMIN. Surely. You are 300 million people in the European Community. I think you can squeeze in a dozen more.

OLIVER. You know that's not the point.

YASMIN. No, the point is that this country wants to join the Western Club, and you won't let them in unless their eastern border is made watertight. So we are chased by dogs and helicopters, and you are in your present – situation, so she can enter European Union. Is this not true?

LEO. Hey. You know what I resent?

Pause. YASMIN *turns to* LEO.

YASMIN. No. What do you resent?

LEO. Two things.

YASMIN. Do please proceed.

LEO. First thing, is all this 'you'. I'm not the European community. I am not even the government of the United States.

YASMIN. Well, this is true.

LEO. And second thing – I'm sorry, three things – second is that although I'm not my government, I would point out that in the last two centuries it's generally agreed that government has been pretty damned hospitable to strangers from beyond its shores. To other country's – huddled masses, yearning to breathe free.

Pause.

YASMIN. So, yes?

LEO. It's a poem, carved on the Statue of Liberty in New York harbour.

YASMIN. Yes, I know. I was waiting for the third thing.

LEO. Oh, yes. Third, you know, it would be nice also if we knew your names. Like, you know ours. You changed them, as you may recall. To those of a Pakistani, an Azeri and a Kurd. Which I know is something of a habit in this region. Wasn't it Bulgaria made their Turks change not just their own names, but their fathers'? Posthumously?

ANTONIO. What, like the Americans gave their slaves names like 'Witherspoon' and 'Pettigrew'?

LEO. So now I'm a slave-owner?

YASMIN. And, actually, Abdul is Afghan. But do you know what *I* resent? About the western intellectuals?

Slight pause.

LEO. Do please proceed.

YASMIN. It is not those who say the west does nothing wrong, because that is so self-evidentally absurd. No, it is liberals who say that west alone *knows* it does wrong. And when Bulgarians oppress their Turks, or Turks their Kurds, it's because they are but infants and the grown-up west must fatherly forgive them for they know not what they do. That it is only western countries who have reached the age of criminal responsibility. The western European tradition as world superego. The universal moral measure of all things.

LEO. Well there you go again.

YASMIN. Where do I go?

LEO. I'm not a western European. I'm an American of mixed Polish and Lithuanian descent.

YASMIN. So do you speak it? Polish? Lithuanian?

LEO. No of course I don't.

YASMIN. Or Hebrew?

LEO. I live in Ithaca, New York. Hebrew is the language of a country in the middle east.

YASMIN. Or for that matter any language but your own?

Slight pause.

LEO. Yuh, as it happens, I do speak a little Spanish. The third world language in our hemisphere.

YASMIN. Doubtless enough to say 'please make up the spare room'.

LEO. Oh please.

YASMIN. But you know the most delicious irony? That it is the west itself exposes its own ignorance and hypocrisy for everyone to see. In the time of the crusades, the Muslim armies exchanged Christian prisoners for Christian books. Because, perhaps, they realised it is preferable to know your enemy than to hold him. And indeed from then to now, by all the means whereby you have invaded us – from the star of Bethlehem to satellite TV – you have taught us oh so much much more of you than you will ever take the pains to learn of us.

Slight pause.

LEO. Well, sure, I take the point –

The telephone rings. The Russian MARINA, who is nearest, answers.

MARINA (*Russian*). Da? Nye veshayete troobkoo. [Yes? Hold on please.]

She holds out the phone to YASMIN. YASMIN to the HOSTAGES as she goes to take the call:

YASMIN. My name is Yasmin. I am a stateless Palestinian. Before that I had residency in Kuwait, but then 'you' came to rescue us. Fair exchange?

She goes and takes the phone.

Hello?

Slight pause.

No I'm sorry. There is no-one speaks your language. You will have to talk in English.

Slight pause.

We will both speak slowly. That is fine.

OLIVER *to* LEO.

OLIVER. Well done.

LEO. What for?

OLIVER. Your little aria. Well, fingers crossed they may decide not to kill us after all.

YASMIN. Yes, 'Oliver' is fine.

LEO. Oh please.

YASMIN. Yes, and 'Gabriella, Toni, and Leonard' are just fine as well.

YASMIN *continues to converse. During this,* CLEOPATRA *approaches the* HOSTAGES, *with her notebook.*

OLIVER. Remind me. What was it Gabriella wasn't to shut out? 'All the other voices in the world – in all their rich variety'?

LEO. Yuh, sure, the irony did not escape me.

YASMIN. So, now, we have exhausted all the social pleasantries, maybe we can proceed to our demands?

GABRIELLA (*to* OLIVER). Hey, you are wrong. We are not prisoners.

OLIVER. Oh, no?

GABRIELLA. You remember poem? We are 'involuntary guests'.

OLIVER (*wryly*). If not, 'involuntary hosts'.

CLEOPATRA. Excuse please. Is this how maybe you write down 'damnosspitable'?

The HOSTAGES *turn to* CLEOPATRA. YASMIN *has been talking both down the phone and, via* ABDUL, *to* RAIF.

TONI. Beg pardon?

CLEOPATRA *shows her book to* GABRIELLA.

CLEOPATRA. See, I write down word. For good vocabulary in English. Take good care vocabulary, grammar she will look behind herself.

GABRIELLA. In fact, it is two word. And I think one 's'. And 'hemisphere' also. But 'Princess' I think two.

YASMIN *has finished her call and is talking to* ABDUL *and* RAIF.

CLEOPATRA. Pop call my infant word for 'Princess'. So we must learn to say so in America.

GABRIELLA *has been affected by the book. So* OLIVER *responds.*

OLIVER. And what's your name?

CLEOPATRA. Is change. First Juanita for my mom. Then Rosa when we are travel much from Hungary. Now pop has gave me new name. Cleopatra.

OLIVER. Blimey.

To prove it, CLEOPATRA *turns her book to the title page.*

CLEOPATRA. No. Is true. Look here.

RAIF *issue orders:* ANTONIO *moves up the ladder, the* WOMEN HOSTAGE-TAKERS *secure the* HOSTAGES *and put hands over their mouths,* ABDUL *leaves* GRIGORI *with the rifle and the armed* RAIF *and* ABDUL *place themselves at the door.*

RAIF (*Russian*). Kharasho. Ani poslali kovo-to. Fsyem pa myestam! [OK. They're sending someone. Everybody to position.]

YASMIN (*Arabic*). kull waaHıd cala makaanuh. [Everybody to the agreed position.]

ABDUL (*Turkish*). Yerlerinize! Susun! [To positions! Silence!]

ANTONIO (*Russian*). Vot on. On i saldat! [He's coming! Him and a soldier!]

RAIF (*Russian*). Oo nyivo zavyazani glaza? [Is he blindfold?]

ANTONIO (*Russian*). Da, zavyazani. Yivo vyedyot saldat. [Yes, he's blindfold. The soldier's leading him.]

YASMIN. What's happening?

ANTONIO. He's with a soldier. The soldier's going back now. He's alone. (*Russian*). Soldat ookhodit.[The soldier's going back now!].

There is a knock at the door. RAIF *looks over to* YASMIN.

YASMIN (*Arabic*). iftaH al-baab. [Open the door.]

ABDUL (*Turkish*). Icheriye gelsin. [Let's admit him.]

The door is opened. BOJOVIC *enters, blindfold, with a small package. The door is quickly closed behind him.*

BOJOVIC (*in the language of our country*). Kazvam se Otets Bojovic. Nosya lekarstvoto. [I am Father Bojovic. I have brought medication.]

RAIF (*Russian*). Pa-rooski gavaritye? [Do you speak Russian?]

BOJOVIC. English is better. I am Father Bojovic. I have medication for Dr Oliver Davenport.

YASMIN. Do you have the answer to our demands?

BOJOVIC. I have – statement. but first I must speak with Dr Davenport. And Mrs Pecs and Miss – uh, um . . . and Professor Katz.

YASMIN. This is the medication?

BOJOVIC. Yes. Where is Dr Davenport?

YASMIN *nods to* FATIMA. *The hands are taken off the* HOSTAGES' *mouths. This dialogue is translated into Russian by* GRIGORI *and* AMIRA.

OLIVER. Uh, here I am.

BOJOVIC. Are you all right?

OLIVER. Well . . .

GABRIELLA. You have his medication?

BOJOVIC. Yes, of course. I must say, there is shortage of all medication in our country. We must fly from Rimini. So instructions I'm so sorry in Italian.

Meanwhile GRIGORI *has been translating to* NICO.

GRIGORI (*Russian*) On prinyos lekarstva dlya Doctora Davenporta. [He has brought the medicine for Dr Davenport.]

BOJOVIC. But presumably you are used as well –

OLIVER. Oh yes.

BOJOVIC. So here it is.

He doesn't know where OLIVER *is.* YASMIN *gestures to* ABDUL *not to let* OLIVER *step forward. She tries to take the package.*

YASMIN. Thank you.

BOJOVIC. I'm sorry. I must give this package direct to Dr Davenport.

GRIGORI *continues to whisper in Russian*:

GRIGORI. On dolzhen atdat pakyet doktoroo Davenportoo. [He must give the package to Dr Davenport.]

YASMIN. You give it to me.

BOJOVIC. But I must say this is not arranged.

GRIGORI (*to* NICO). On gavarit shto ab etom nye dagavarilis. [He says this was not arranged.]

YASMIN. Oh I am so sorry. Perhaps if you permit us to call out as well as you call in our arrangements might prove more equitable.

RAIF *gestures to* YASMIN *not to lose her temper.*

YASMIN. We have no time for games. You give the package to the hostage after you respond to our demands.

BOJOVIC *senses* REFUGEES *gathering and is getting flustered.*

BOJOVIC. I – um, I am empowered only –

ANTONIO (*impatient*). Food. Transport. Permit.

BOJOVIC. Yes, when Dr Davenport, there will be food –

ABDUL (*Arabic*). tosreeH ᶜamal? [Work permit?]

YASMIN. And work permit.

BOJOVIC. And also I am safe return of course –

YASMIN. Of course.

BOJOVIC. And you tell what food you want –

ANTONIO. But main demand. Transport. Work permits.

GRIGORI (*to* NICO, *whispering in Russian*). Antonio tryebooyet yediy, transporta, dakoomyentaf. [Antonio's demanding food, transport and documents.]

BOJOVIC. Yes. On – main demand –

YASMIN. They do, they tell you what to say?

BOJOVIC. Yes. yes. But you must understand. I am not lawyer. I am simple priest. You are demanding priest in blindfold. Here I am.

Pause. AMIRA *intervenes.*

AMIRA. Please, father. Take your time.

BOJOVIC. I must ask. I must hear voice of Mrs Pecs and Professor Katz. And um, Miss Um.

YASMIN. Feel free.

As the HOSTAGES *reply,* AMIRA *tells* MARINA *what's been happening*:

AMIRA (*Russian*). On prinyos lekarstva dlya Doktora Davenporta. Antonio tryebooyet yediy, transporta i dokoomenta. On nye yoorist. Prastoi svyashchennik. [He's brought medication for Dr Davenport. Antonio demanded food, transport and documents. He says he isn't a lawyer, simply a priest.]

Meanwhile:

GABRIELLA (*in the language of our country*). Kazvam se Gabriella Pecs. [I am Gabriella Pecs.]

BOJOVIC. I dobre ste? [And you're all right?]

GABRIELLA. Oh, hunkydory.

BOJOVIC. Professor Katz?

LEO. OK. As Olly said.

BOJOVIC. And Miss –

TONI. Miss Newsome. Fine. I'd just like to thank my agent and please send my best to all at Number 32. And I'd murder for a bacon lettuce and tomato sandwich.

This expression is slightly mystifying to some people.

BOJOVIC. Thank you.

BOJOVIC *has regained composure.*

You demand one that all asylum seekers grant asylum and work permit in country of their choice.

GRIGORI (*translates quietly to* NICO). Miy fsye tryebooyem oobyezhishcha i razresheniya na rabotoo. [We are all asking for asylum and work permits.]

Meanwhile:

YASMIN. Yes?

BOJOVIC. I must say this hard demand for government of this one country to concede I think.

ANTONIO. I don't believe this.

AMIRA (*whispers to* MARINA). On gavarit shto eta trebovaniye ochen seryoznoye. [He is saying this is a very serious demand.]

YASMIN. You have had a whole day to consult the governments of other countries.

BOJOVIC. Also this country and all governments of western countries signing international convention on asylum seekers, which lay down procedure for consideration of these problems.

ABDUL (*Arabic*). weysh yagool? [What is he saying?]

YASMIN. This cannot be serious.

BOJOVIC. However.

Slight pause.

There are provisions also of – of 1950-something international law on refugee. Which if – a person prove he risk political or race or religious persecution, he can stay in country.

GRIGORI (*translates to* NICO). Yest myezhdoonarodniy zakon . . . [There is an international law . . .]

YASMIN. I think that is 1952.

AMIRA (*translates to* MARINA). No, yest myezhdoonarodniy zakon . . . [There is an international law . . .]

BOJOVIC. So what I must ask you, for list of all identity, your country, reason for departing, and country of your choice to enter. Oh, and passport number. And this matter then will be resolve as quickly as maybe.

GRIGORI (*translates*). Miy dalzhniy skazat yemoo, familii, grazhdanstvo, prichiny viyyezda. On gavarit, shto vapros boodyet reshon, pa vazmozhnasti biystra . . . [We must tell him our names, country, reason for departing, then he says the matter will be resolved as quickly as possible.]

ANTONIO. Names?

RAIF. Passport?

YASMIN. This is not possible.

BOJOVIC. You make demand you want work permit in country of your choice. Sooner or later, you must choose I think.

Pause as YASMIN *whispers via* ABDUL *to* RAIF *and to* ANTONIO; *and* AMIRA *to the Russian speakers.*

AMIRA (*whispers to* MARINA). Miy dalzhni skazat yemoo prichiny viyyezda i stranoo kooda miy khatim viyyekhat. [We must tell him our reason for departing and the country we wish to enter.]

Meanwhile, GRIGORI *is grabbed by* NICO.

NICO (*kind of Polish*). Nazywam sie Nico. To jest moja córka, Kleopatra, a to jej dziecko. Jesteśmy z Bośni. Nie mamy paszportów. (Nazyvam shem Nico. To yest moya tchurka Cleopatra, a to yey djetsko. Yesteshmee zzz Boshnee. Niye mamee pashportuv.) [My name is Nico. This is my daughter Cleopatra and her baby. We are from Bosnia. We have no passports.]

Meanwhile, ANTONIO *to* BOJOVIC:

ANTONIO. Not everyone has passport.

BOJOVIC. Well, I guess ID.

YASMIN. Even ID.

ANTONIO. And we are not arrested?

BOJOVIC. No. No, there is amnesty.

ABDUL (*Turkish, to* RAIF). Aff çıkhtıgını mı söyledi? [Did he say, there was an amnesty.]

Another brief moment of consultation. AMIRA *has continued to speak to* MARINA:

AMIRA (*whispers*). On gavarit shto vapros boodyet reshon pa vazmozhnosti biystra. [He says the matter will be settled as quickly as possible.]

Meanwhile NICO *has continued to brief* GRIGORI, *including:*

NICO. Najprzót Serbowie, a potem Węgrzy dali nam papiery, ale my wyrzucilismy je. Jesteśmy cyganami, starym narodę. A teraz jesteśmy ofiarami oczyszczenia etnycznego przez Kroatów. (Nighpshrut Serboviye, a pottem Vengzhry dali nam papiery, alleh mi vyshuchillishmy yay. Yesteshme tzyganamee, starhim naroden. A teraz yesteshme offyarami ochchischenia etnichnego pshez Kroatov.) [We have no passports. The Serbs gave us papers, and then the Hungarians, but we threw them away. Now we are victim of ethnic cleansing by Croats.]

Meanwhile:

BOJOVIC. Please what happens now?

YASMIN. All right. We make a list. No names, just initials. No passport numbers. But we will all write down the name of our country, what has driven us to leave it and where we want to go.

Somewhat unwillingly, GRIGORI *is pushed forward by* NICO.

GRIGORI. This man. He is call Nico and his daughter Cleopatra and her baby.

NICO. Jesteśmy z Bośni. (Yesteshmee zzzBoshnee.) [We are Bosnian.]

GRIGORI. They say they Bosnian. They have no passport. They are give Serb passport. This they throw away.

AMIRA translates:

AMIRA (*whispers to* MARINA). On abyasnyayet shto sloochilas. [He's explaining what happened.]

NICO *prompts* GRIGORI:

NICO. Papiery wyrzucilismy. (Papiery vyshuchillishmy.) [Papers thrown away.]

GRIGORI. Then they are give Hungarian ID, but they are not Hungarians. Why should they have this paper? So they throw away too.

NICO. Jesteśmy cyganami, starym narodę. (Yesteshme tzyganamee, starhim naroden.) [We are gypsies, an ancient people.]

More prompting from NICO. GRIGORI *continues, unconvincingly.*

GRIGORI. This family gypsy. They most ancient people. They come from ancient time in India, they travel all of world.

NICO. Flamenco.

GRIGORI. Yes, they invent flamenco dance and pots found they bring from England to Bulgaria.

NICO. Flamenco.

GRIGORI. I say flamenco already.

NICO. Za Hitlera. (Za Heetlera.)

GRIGORI. They many of thousands killed by Hitler but they give no compensation like Israelis.

NICO. Jesteśmy z Bośni. (Yesteshmee zzzBoshnee.) [We are Bosnian.]

NICO *goes to fetch* CLEOPATRA. GRIGORI, *lowering his voice:*

GRIGORI. They say they Bosnia and ethnic cleaned by Serb.

NICO. Ne, Kroaty! (Nye, Kroatov!)

GRIGORI. No, sorry, Croat. They speak I think a kind of Polish. I think they are usari gyspy. But they say Bosnia.

NICO *returns with* CLEOPATRA *and the baby.*

NICO. Sprzedać dziecko za dobrą cenę. (Spshedach dietsko za dobrom tsenen.) [Sell baby for good price.]

GRIGORI (*unhappily*). Oh, and they prepare to sell small baby to good family in western country. With good price. So they do not come with hollow hand to Germany.

AMIRA (*whispers to* MARINA). On gavarit shto on khochet pradat rebyonka. [He says he wants to sell the baby.]

OLIVER (*whispers*). Usari?

GABRIELLA (*whispers*). Scum.

TONI (*whispers*). She says she'll sell her baby?

YASMIN. Right. We make a list. No names. No papers.

Arabic, to FATIMA:

utliqee yadeyh aHsan. [You'd better untie his hands.]

She takes BOJOVIC'*s arm and leads him to* OLIVER.

Now, here is Dr Davenport.

BOJOVIC. He is here?

OLIVER. Yes, I'm here.

BOJOVIC *gives him the package.*

Thank you. That's a great relief.

He gestures to the effect that he can't give the injection unless they untie his hands.

YASMIN (*Arabic, to* ABDUL). khud hal-wara'a wuktub ᶜaleyha tafaaseelak ash-shakhseeya. [Here is some paper for you to write down your details.]

As ABDUL *unties* OLIVER'*s hands, the* REFUGEES *huddle round drawing up their histories. They are writing on computer paper from the workstation.* FATIMA *will call upon* ABDUL *and* YASMIN'*s help to draw up her submission.*

TONI. Why don't they have fucking passports, for Christ's sake? If they're trying to emigrate?

LEO. Well, I guess that some of them come from countries where they don't issue them to everybody.

GABRIELLA. Also, I think, if you will arrive in west illegally, it will be better with no passport, so nowhere deport you to.

OLIVER *is immersed in the instructions in the package, which contains a phial of insulin and a hypodermic.* NICO *is convinced he is being overlooked by others, as if it's an exam. He summons* CLEOPATRA *to go further afield. They go out to another corner of the church.* GRIGORI, *with his completed 'form', has approached* BOJOVIC. *He speaks quietly:*

GRIGORI. Father. I must explain. My name is Grigori Kolorenko. I from Ukraine. But by birth I am German.

BOJOVIC. Yes?

GRIGORI. Yes, you see, my mother she of German ancestry. My real name not Grigori but Gyor.

GRIGORI *turns to see* ANTONIO *watching him suspiciously. He lowers his voice but carries on lobbying* BOJOVIC.

LEO. What's that guy saying?

GABRIELLA. He claim he German.

LEO. And that helps?

GABRIELLA. Not half. Everybody German can go back. No matter if they leave in fifteen century. Just like Israel.

GRIGORI has finished his pitch.

BOJOVIC. I do my best.

GRIGORI. Thank you, father.

He moves away.

LEO. In the war, the judge was saying, there were kids, being transported to some camp or other, so starved they ate their name tags. For the cardboard.

GABRIELLA. In Hermitage, art gallery in Leningrad, where you know they have siege for two winters, curators live on jelly made from restoration glue.

NICO *appears from the gloom of the rest of the church, and gives a big 'psst' to* AMIRA, *who follows him back out.*

GABRIELLA. But this does not mean I think they have therefore right of entry to nice country of their choice for all time since.

OLIVER (*reading*). Forgive me?

YASMIN *and* RAIF *have collected the 'forms' and are passing the* HOSTAGES *en route to* BOJOVIC. YASMIN *notices that* OLIVER *has not taken his shot.*

YASMIN. So is this not OK?

OLIVER. It's fine.

YASMIN. It is the right stuff?

OLIVER. Yes. I'm just putting off the evil moment.

Slight pause.

Ever since I was a boy.

YASMIN *shakes her head dismissively. They turn to go to* BOJOVIC. ANTONIO *is watching* OLIVER *closely;* GRIGORI *among the* REFUGEES *listening.*

YASMIN. All done. OK.

LEO. Good luck.

YASMIN. You wish us 'Good luck'?

LEO. Yuh. Is that a shock to you?

YASMIN *turns away, perhaps moving a little towards* BOJOVIC *before she suddenly turns back, waving the applications.*

YASMIN. OK. You wish to know these people. Fine.

She is turning the pages of the sheaf of applications.

This is – A.R., the Bosnian, she plays the cello in the orchestra in Banja Luka, but due to – changing circumstances she decides for safety to move down to Sarajevo. And – what's this?

RAIF (*reading the Russian*). Marina. Uh – Riga.

YASMIN. Oh, yes. This woman, who as I gather lives in Lithuania or Latvia since half her life but is denied the vote because she's Russian. And this is, AA?

ANTONIO. Me.

YASMIN. Of course, Antonio, who is student at Patrice Lumumba University in Moscow. And once upon a time he lives in a . . .

She can't read the writing.

ANTONIO. A dormitory.

YASMIN. Aha, with fifty other Africans and they are besieged by fellow students – good heroic Russian internationalists – and he decides to emigrate to western Europe, and ends up in a – squatter camp? just outside Paris which the police break up because they need the land to build the National Library. And so heyho he is deported back, not in fact to Russia but to –

ANTONIO. Poland.

YASMIN. Where he enters into an 'indeterminate condition' where he remains until today. While – T – is – Sri Lankan? who is, goes as maid to – ah, Kuwait – where the citizens are not known themselves to lift anything heavier than money. Where she is beaten and from which she presumably escapes to . . . be a 'disco dancer' in the Hot Banana Club in Cyprus. Limassol.

She notes missing forms. To RAIF, *in Arabic:*

weyn al-ghajar? [Where are the gypsies?] (*English.*) Gypsies?

RAIF (*Azeri*). Gidib bakhajaaım. [I'll go and look.]

RAIF *goes.* YASMIN *gestures with his form, which is next.*

YASMIN. And that is Raif, who is Azeri and also has a tale to tell. First, he loses his right leg doing his internationalist duty and fighting mediaeval obscurantism in Afghanistan. Then he's demobilised and earns his living taking flowers from Baku to sell in Moscow till he is threatened so much by the Chechen mafia he returns home to Azerbaijan, just in time to find his father, exactly as the Armenians had left him, surrounded by his luggage, at the entrance to his village and without his face.

LEO. I'm sorry?

YASMIN. You know, like Red Indians?

LEO. Jesus Christ.

YASMIN. Oh, and that is Abdul, who may well be himself a mediaeval obscurantist, but who doubtless feels that almost anywhere is preferable to contemporary Kabul. So, do you know enough?

RAIF *reappears from his search, and shrugs.*

YASMIN (*Arabic*). laazim hown weyn makaan hummi. [They must be somewhere.]

GRIGORI takes the opportunity for a confidential word with OLIVER.

GRIGORI. It is not true.

OLIVER. What?

GRIGORI. There are no massacre of Azeri villages. Is Muslim propaganda.

YASMIN has come across another piece of paper.

YASMIN. Oh, now you look there. While you are busy making Kuwait safe for democracy and freedom. It is in English. We help her write it down.

She hands the paper to OLIVER, then takes the other papers to BOJOVIC as OLIVER looks at the paper. Its contents disturb him.

GABRIELLA. What does it say?

OLIVER. She's a Kurd. She is born in would you credit Batman Turkey but her family moves south to avoid the persecution. Having moved, her father and her aunt are gassed and killed at – Halabja? – in 1988. In 1989 her husband emigrates to Austria and leaves her with their child. Her brother is conscripted to the Iraqi army and refuses. He is taken to a camp and three months later he turns up a half-wit with one eye. She is by this time in the mountains but decides to take her brother back to – Qala Diza? where her mother now lives with her son. When they arrive. When they arrive.

Slight pause.

She finds . . .

He hands the paper to TONI. Pause.

I think. I can give myself a small injection.

He looks up at ANTONIO who is watching; OLIVER thinks because of the Kurdish paper. As TONI looks at the paper, OLIVER tries to find a vein.

TONI. I'm wearing her clothes.

OLIVER slips and stabs himself.

OLIVER. *Ow.*

ANTONIO. You OK?

OLIVER. Yes. I'm sorry, I –

ANTONIO. You sorry? Why? Whatever for?

ANTONIO goes and picks up OLIVER's package of equipment.

So you are diabetes, right?

OLIVER. That's right.

ANTONIO. And so you do this everyday?

OLIVER *nods.* ANTONIO *is looking at the printed instructions.*

ANTONIO. What is the phrase – 'preferring you to me'?

OLIVER. Um – 'rather you than me'.

ANTONIO. Oh, yes. And you speak Italian?

OLIVER. They send – they have to send –

ANTONIO. But still – you speak Italian.

Slight pause. REFUGEES *are beginning to gather round this quiet interrogation.*

OLIVER. Yup.

ANTONIO. What does this say?

OLIVER. Oh, you know. The usual chemist's – pharmacist's, instructions.

ANTONIO. Yes?

OLIVER. So many – dosage. Keep from children, all that stuff.

ANTONIO (*pointing to a particular sentence*). What is this saying?

OLIVER. It says – 'not to be taken orally'. That means, by the mouth.

ANTONIO. Which is the word for 'orally'?

Pause. OLIVER *can't keep it up. He closes his eyes.*

ANTONIO. What does it really say?

Pause.

OLIVER. It says, the insulin is a harmless salt solution. And it tells us – sforzo, that all *efforts* are being made for our release, negotiations are proceeding, we must stay – composto? oh, composed. Collected. And they – plan to cut the lights and the water and the heat at nightfall. Oh, and they ask if you know about the painting.

OLIVER *hands the 'instructions' back to* ANTONIO, *who looks inquisitive.*

That's the painting up there on the wall. Covered by the bandage.

ANTONIO (*pointing to another section*). And this? What does this say?

Slight pause.

OLIVER. 'The bug is in the spare cartridge'.

LEO. Oh, Jesus.

ANTONIO (*Russian*). Yest padslooshka. [There's a bug.]

Immediate reaction from the REFUGEES. BOJOVIC *too works out the implications of this discovery.* RAIF *takes the cartridge from* OLIVER, *and looks at it.*

BOJOVIC. I think now, I will like to go.

This draws general attention to him.

I must say I know naturally nothing of all this.

Pause.

I am safe return. Then I think that naturally food must be sent in quickly.

Slight pause. AMIRA *has reappeared with* NICO *and* CLEOPATRA.

AMIRA. No need. Look what my friends maybe of Bosnia are finding here.

NICO *and* CLEOPATRA *carry armfuls of potatoes, bags of dried fish and rice, pulses and firewood. The* GYPSIES *dump their treasures, with a huge clatter, in the centre of the church.* NICO *marches over to present his application to* BOJOVIC.

NICO (*kind of Polish*). Prosze księdza, tu są nasze papiery. Prosze zrozumiec ze jesteśmy z Bozni-Hercegowinji. (Proshe kshienndza, tu sown nashe papyery. Proshe zrozoomyiyech ze yesteshmi zzzBoshnee-Hertsegoveenee.) [Father. Here are our forms. Please understand we are from Bosnia Herccgovina.]

He kisses BOJOVIC's *hand.* BOJOVIC *has realised the discovery of the food has revoked his passport.*

BOJOVIC. Now I must say – I insist –

YASMIN. Oh yes. Please go. We have no desire to harm one hair of the head of a Minister of the Holy One True Church.

She goes and takes FATIMA's *form from* TONI *and gives it to* BOJOVIC.

ANTONIO (*Russian*). Fsyem pa myestam. (Everybody into position.)

ANTONIO *goes up the ladder,* ABDUL *to the door. The* HOSTAGES *are being held and silenced in preparation for the door being opened.*

YASMIN. But I'm afraid you are the last. We wish no more nice friendly visitors with little secrets up their sleeves. And you will please inform your friends – we need a guarantee that everyone will be admitted to the country of their choice. And if we have no such guarantee by – six o'clock tomorrow morning, we will kill a hostage. Most likely it will be the Zionist Professor Katz. So get him out of here.

LEO (*bleakly*). Hey. Look –

A hand is slapped over his mouth. RAIF *escorts* BOJOVIC – *none too gently – to the door.*

ABDUL (*to* YASMIN, *joking, in Arabic*). mish laazim tudkhuleehum illa iza hum ᶜaryaaneen. [You should admit them naked.]

YASMIN. Oh, yes, why not?

YASMIN *speaks straight into* BOJOVIC*'s face.*

There is one exception to the rule. We will admit you. Or another Priest of the Holy One True Church. But only without sleeves. Like the Risen Christ of Michelangelo. Stark bollock naked.

Laughter, and perhaps a little more, as this is translated.
ANTONIO *signals the all clear to* RAIF *who opens the door for* BOJOVIC *to be pushed through by* RAIF*. The door is closed and locked.* YASMIN *turns back to the* HOSTAGES*. Hands are removed from their mouths. A long silence.*

YASMIN. Or maybe the first will be Dr Diabetic Davenport with his distressing ailments and fluent technical Italian.

YASMIN *marches over to* OLIVER*. To* ABDUL*, Arabic:*

huwwa kassar jihaaz attasonnut? [Did he destroy the bug?]

ABDUL (*to* RAIF*, Turkish*). O dinleme jihaazı qırdın mı? [Did you destroy the bug?]

RAIF (*Azeri*). Haalaa gırajaaım onu. [No, but I will.]

RAIF *takes the cartridge, finds a hammer, and gets smashing.*

YASMIN. Who having kindly told us all about his friends out there and their nice plans for us –

OLIVER. They're not –

YASMIN. – will now explain please all about this painting. The one they ask you if we know about. Raif!

She takes the revolver from RAIF*.*

Which now – I think – we will.

YASMIN *is pointing the revolver at* OLIVER*. He is scared.*

OLIVER. Um, look – look, please –

YASMIN. I mean, one must imagine it is something fairly special, for two great art historians to come all this way, with all this magnificent technology.

OLIVER. Well, actually, in fact –

YASMIN. But now I think we should know quite how special. Or perhaps, to show that we mean business –

OLIVER. Please –

GABRIELLA (*quickly*). In fact, it actually not so special.

YASMIN *looks to* GABRIELLA*.*

GABRIELLA. In fact, it just ordinary church painting.

YASMIN *gestures witheringly at the equipment.*

GABRIELLA. Which we think at first is maybe painted very long ago, and is first of its kind in all world, and therefore yes a little bit damn special. But, actually, we find that it turn out –

LEO. – to be exactly what you thought it was.

GABRIELLA *looks at* LEO *in horror.*

LEO. I mean, come on, let's not try to pull one over on these people.

GABRIELLA. Leo –

LEO. I mean, they'll understand why this painting is so valuable. Knowing, as they do, so much more of us than we will ever take the pains to learn of them.

Pause. GABRIELLA *looks desperately at* OLIVER, *who can't do anything.*

YASMIN. Please do proceed.

LEO (*gesturing with his tied hands*). Sure. If you'd be so kind.

YASMIN *gives a curt nod.* GRIGORI *unties* LEO's *hands.*

LEO. And thus doubtless won't need telling that about the beginning of the 14th century there was a mighty change nay turnaround in the way that western painters chose to address the world around them. Which, although it technically consisted of a number of devices to render the effect of three dimensions on a flat plane, was essentially a key step in the growing understanding, or belief, that not God but Man is the measure of all things. That his point of vision is *the* point of vision. That there is no outside authority defining or pre-empting what he sees, with his own restless, questing, yearning, endlessly inquisitive two eyes.

He's at the photograph of the Giotto Lamentation.

And it has been argued that the starting point of that, the first leg of the race from God to Man, was run by this guy, Giotto di Bondone, in 1300-ish in Northern Italy. But what these guys have discovered is that in fact by then the first lap was already run. Right here. Up there. So people, what you have here is not just the most valuable art-find of the century, but, to coin a phrase, the birth of universal European man.

He looks questioningly at GABRIELLA.

GABRIELLA. I think I say of modern rational universal man.

LEO. Well you do too. Which is of course the *most* delicious irony. That the folks out there, who want so badly to be universal Europeans, to be part of that, are much more interested in that than they are in you, or even us. So they'll bar their gates to you, and risk our lives, to keep the art. For Christ's sake: 'Do they know about the painting?'. And it's not the first time. As Dubrovnik burns, western intellectuals write polite letters to the papers protesting the destruction of the architecture. Mitterand destroys a squatter camp to build a library. The camp guards at Auschwitz spend their evenings listening to Mozart on the gramophone.

Pause.

And of course, it can be argued that you shouldn't blame the art. But on the other hand . . . there is a view, that somewhere in all that remorseless questioning – there is – as you point out – a kind of arrogance. That somehow it's always Western man who's doing the inquisiting, and everybody else who's quisited. So maybe, yuh, there *is* some line, if not from Beethoven to Buchenwald, then at least to the World Bank, the IMF and NATO.

Slight pause. Half to OLIVER *and* GABRIELLA.

Which is a view I find increasingly persuasive. Actually.

A moment. Then:

So hey. You know what I'd do? I would write a statement, addressing this – this intriguing double standard. And I'd insist it gets put out on the radio. And I'd say that if it isn't, then you'll douse that S.O.B. in gasoline and fry it off the wall.

Slight pause. As if an afterthought:

Hey, even better. As you say, there's a tradition of exchanging prisoners for books. Well, we're not nearly so valuable to you as that is. So, hell, why not underline the irony. And set your – huddled masses free.

There is a silence.

AMIRA. This is painting here?

LEO. That's right. Under the canvas. In fact, before they cut the water off, you could remove the facing. Take a look at what you got.

A moment. AMIRA *goes up the ladder, to the painting. She touches it.*

AMIRA. How do you take this off?

LEO. With water. And a little – tender loving care.

YASMIN *quickly to* ABDUL *and* RAIF.

YASMIN (*Arabic*). ᶜul-luh hannaaqish kalaam az-zalami. [Tell him we'll discuss what he said.]

ABDUL (*Turkish*). Söyledikhlerini tartıshmak istiyor. [She wants to discuss what he said.]

ANTONIO (*to* GRIGORI, *Russian*). Atvyedi yivo. [Take him back.]

YASMIN, RAIF, ABDUL *and* ANTONIO *go into a huddle.* AMIRA *looks at the covered painting.* GRIGORI *brings* LEO *back to the other* HOSTAGES. LEO *puts his hands behind his back for tying.* GRIGORI *shrugs and gestures for him to sit. He does so, his hands untied, with a smile on his face.* GRIGORI *like the others is keener on the* HUDDLE *than the* HOSTAGES.

GABRIELLA. What are you doing?

LEO. I am trying to get us out of here.

GABRIELLA. But you put at risk our painting.

LEO. Which if it means anything at all, must surely rate the needs and rights of living human beings higher than what you described – acutely – as a form of currency.

GABRIELLA *shrugs.*

Oh, but I'm sorry. You can't be dumping ground for dregs.

GABRIELLA. Oh, please.

LEO (*to* OLIVER). And of course, all that is based on the idea that works of art might contain some kind of universal moral truth. Well, hush my mouth.

OLIVER. No. Actually, I think you may be right.

Slight pause.

LEO. I'm sorry?

OLIVER. Perhaps there are universal human values which we should protect. From those who threaten them.

LEO *picks up the hypodermic package and gestures with it towards the door of the church.*

LEO. Olly, those fuckers nearly got us killed.

OLIVER *gestures towards the* HOSTAGE-TAKERS.

OLIVER. Oh no. Those fuckers nearly killed us. And still may.

The huddle has split: RAIF *has commandered* GRIGORI *and is calling down* AMIRA *to start writing a statement* YASMIN *arrives at* HOSTAGES, *with* ANTONIO.

YASMIN. OK. We have reached a decision. We will issue a statement, as you so helpfully suggest.

LEO *looks to* OLIVER, *then nods graciously to* YASMIN.

YASMIN. And to underline your irony, sure, we will make a humanitarian gesture. We will let the women go.

Pause. The HOSTAGES *react – or attempt to disguise – their reactions to this news.*

TONI. What, now?

YASMIN. Yes, now.

Slight pause.

TONI. Well, great. Thanks.

To LEO:

And – uh, thanks. I'm –

LEO (*to stop her*). Please.

YASMIN (*Arabic, to* ABDUL, *turning to go*). khalleehum jaahzeen. [Get them ready.]

GABRIELLA. Um – forgive me please.

YASMIN turns back.

YASMIN. Yes? What?

GABRIELLA. If I will say I stay, will you let one of men go?

OLIVER. What?

YASMIN quick eye contact with ANTONIO.

YASMIN. No. No I'm sorry. It is you or no-one.

Again, she turns to go upstage.

GABRIELLA. Well. So be it.

YASMIN turns back.

YASMIN. You – you want to stay?

Slight pause.

GABRIELLA. Not want. I will.

YASMIN. You're sure?

GABRIELLA (*with a shrug*). Voilà.

Pause.

YASMIN. So be it.

To ABDUL, *in Arabic:*

shoof iza kull shee tamaam. [Check if everything's OK.]

ABDUL goes up the ladder. ANTONIO *goes to take* TONI *to the door.*

TONI (*to* GABRIELLA). Hey, have you gone crazy?

GABRIELLA. No.

TONI. Right.

ANTONIO (*to* TONI). Hey. You want your pretty clothe?

He gestures to FATIMA. TONI *looks longingly at her clothes.*

TONI. Well, p'raps . . .

Slight pause.

No. Let her keep 'em.

To OLIVER *and* LEO, *but also, perhaps, to* FATIMA:

And good luck.

YASMIN. You tell them. They call up on the telephone for a statement in – in half an hour.

TONI. Yuh. Sure.

TONI seems almost unwilling to go.

TONI. Hey, guys. I've just remembered number two.

OLIVER. What was it?

TONI. 'Don't make helpful suggestions'.

ABDUL nods the all clear from the ladder. ANTONIO takes TONI to the door. Quickly the door is opened, TONI is pushed through, and it's locked again. Meanwhile, GRIGORI has come forward, with the beginnings of a draft statement in his hands.

GRIGORI. Excuse. We have Paris library and concentration camp. There was a third example, no?

LEO. Dubrovnik.

GRIGORI (*turning to go*). Thank you.

LEO. So could you use some help?

Pause.

YASMIN. Yes. We could use some help.

He goes back upstage. LEO making to follow:

OLIVER. Leo. You heard.

A moment. LEO goes upstage to join the drafting group. There is a moment between OLIVER and GABRIELLA before OLIVER speaks.

OLIVER. Gabri –

GABRIELLA. For three reasons. One is whatever painting really worth, still it is my discovery, and I don't want to see it fry off wall.

OLIVER. But still, you –

GABRIELLA. Two. If it not what we first think, then likely painter from our country. And so I should coco I run out and leave it here.

Slight pause.

As after all said and done, I am curator there if only of Brueghel second cousin. And now of Giotto copy in late Byzantine style.

Pause.

And three: to show that scumbag, even after forty year of botch-ups, forty year of fail to build one wall of new Jerusalem, still we worthless folks can behave – well, little bitty better – braver – than he think we do.

Pause.

OLIVER. I should have been more brave. That stupid business with the cartridge.

GABRIELLA. Hey come on.

Pause.

OLIVER. You know, it was your passion.

GABRIELLA. Sorry?

OLIVER. Why I changed my mind, that evening. And I remember thinking, even then. How pathetically unserious, our – discourse must appear to you.

Slight pause. GABRIELLA *looks at* OLIVER.

How easy it must seem – it is – from the portals of the Ruskin Institute, to claim it's more or less a toss-up between Pride and Prejudice and Police Academy.

Slight pause.

To those who do our dirty work. Who have stood on Europe's battlements for all those years.

Pause. GABRIELLA *takes* OLIVER*'s hands.*

GABRIELLA. Okeydoke. Fourth reason. If I cannot leave here painting, how do you presume I can leave you?

Scene Six

Shortly before dawn. The church is lit with candles and the dying fires on which food has been cooked and round which HOSTAGES and REFUGEES are sat to keep warm. The facing of the painting has been removed, but in the darkness we can see little of it. There is some nervousness in the air. YASMIN is playing with a set of keys. AMIRA has taken her cello from its case. ABDUL is with RAIF. There is tension between LEO, OLIVER and GABRIELLA, which LEO resolves to address.

LEO. 'God bless Vespuccia'.

OLIVER. I beg your pardon?

TUNU *is coming to the* HOSTAGES *to collect their plates.* GRIGORI *starts to listen to the conversation.*

LEO. An idle speculation. Whether things might have gone differently, had they chosen our beloved founder's surname rather than his first name.

Slight pause.

OLIVER. 'Vespuccia the Beautiful'.

LEO. Well, exactly.

GABRIELLA. 'As Vespuccian as apple pie'.

LEO. 'The House Un-Vespuccian Activities Committee'.

OLIVER. Promoting naturally 'life, liberty and the Vespuccian way'.

GRIGORI. Hey. Or maybe. 'All-Vespuccian Girl'.

Slight pause.

LEO. Hey. Right.

TUNU takes the plates. OLIVER calls after her.

OLIVER. Excuse me, what's the time?

TUNU looks to YASMIN, who shakes her head.

GRIGORI. Actually –

YASMIN. No.

GRIGORI shrugs. YASMIN goes a little way apart.

OLIVER. Just, it would be nice to know. How long we have before they take up your suggestion. And fry our painting off the wall.

LEO. Hey. Olly.

AMIRA doesn't see why the HOSTAGES shouldn't know the time. She puts down her cello and comes down to them.

OLIVER. Hello.

AMIRA. Hello.

Slight pause.

Your painting. Look like window.

OLIVER. Yes.

AMIRA. So many star.

Slight pause.

Is good word 'star'. Our word is 'zvezda'. Ugly word I think.

GABRIELLA. Is same for us.

Slight pause AMIRA takes out some photographs from her wallet to show to the HOSTAGES.

AMIRA. This my mother.

A moment, then GABRIELLA takes the picture to look at it.

AMIRA. This my father with my sister. This string section of our orchestra, in trip to Prague. Our big night out.

The HOSTAGES look at AMIRA's pictures.

OLIVER. Perhaps – you'll play for us.

AMIRA is shaking her head as YASMIN appears. ABDUL and RAIF are sharing a joke.

YASMIN. What's going on?

LEO. We were asking if she'd play for us.

AMIRA shrugs and shakes her head.

YASMIN. And what are these?

GABRIELLA. Just photographs.

AMIRA. Of better days.

She is gathering her pictures up.

LEO. So why d'you leave?

Slight pause.

AMIRA. Terrible things.

She stands.

GABRIELLA. 'Lora'. In our old language word for star is 'lora'.

AMIRA. It is ten minutes before five.

AMIRA *goes upstage.*

OLIVER. An hour to go.

We hear RAIF *finishing his joke.*

RAIF (*Azeri*). Adam da dedi ki, bakh, daha shimdiden bazaarlıkh yapıyorsun. [And so the man said, see, you're haggling already.]

YASMIN, *angry, strides to* RAIF *and* ABDUL.

YASMIN. What is this? (*Arabic.*) rijaa'an, eysh biseer hown? [What is going on please?]

ABDUL. (*Arabic.*) huwwa yimzaH faqat. [It's just a joke.]

YASMIN. (*Arabic.*) irweelna fa'izan, salleena kullna. [You tell it please? Amuse us all?]

ABDUL. (*Arabic.*) yagool innoo maafee moomisaat fee . . . [It is about there being no prostitutes . . .] (*English.*) OK. No hooker in USSR . . .

YASMIN. I see.

ANTONIO *gestures to* YASMIN *to cool it.*

GRIGORI (*Russian*). Ya shootkoo znayoo. [I know a joke.]

AMIRA (*gesturing that he should include the* HOSTAGES). Grigori.

GRIGORI (*in English*). I know great joke. In village remote corner of Siberia, where they see pig for first time. One say is overfeeding rat. Another say, is starving cow. Third say, maybe rat who strive that he develop into cow.

There's something not quite right about the joke.

Or she.

That hasn't cracked it.

It is joke how peasant backwardness counter by revolutionary optimism. Now maybe bit more irony. Sorry.

Pause.

ANTONIO. Hey. Like – violonchel?

AMIRA. Cello.

ANTONIO. Like guitar who want to grow up to be double bass.

Laughter.

So where you play? Jazz band?

AMIRA *shakes her head.*

ANTONIO (*Russian, to* RAIF). Djaz-banda nyetoo. [No jazz band.]

RAIF. Maybe rock and roll.

ANTONIO. One for money, two for show. Three to get ready –

RAIF (*sings*). Three to get ready now Blue Suede Shoes.

ANTONIO *is moving to the cello to hand it to* AMIRA.

AMIRA. No, no.

To change the subject:

But I tell joke. No, story. Once there was and there was not a Padisah – great ruler, who must go off to battle, leaving three lovely daughters back behind.

CLEOPATRA *is translating to* NICO, *who becomes increasingly agitated.*

AMIRA. And he tell them, while that he is gone, they may go anywhere in all the palace and its gardens, but they are forbid to enter one room at the very back and on right hand side. Else there will be great harm.

CLEOPATRA. Excuse excuse.

AMIRA. Yes please?

NICO (*kind of Polish*). Historia nie tak idzie. (Historiya nyc tak idzhe.) [The story is wrong.]

CLEOPATRA. Is not right story.

AMIRA. Oh?

NICO (*waving at* GRIGORI *to translate*). W prawdziwej historji jest syn i corką i – fudhopp (Y pravdiviy historiyi yest syn i tchurka i – fudhopp.) [In the real story it is a son and daughter and a woodcutter.]

GRIGORI. In real story, apparently, it one daughter and one son of – fudhopp?

NICO (*miming vigorously*). Fudhopp.

GRIGORI (*realising it's the English word*). Oh, woodchopper.

AMIRA *allows* NICO *to take over the story.*

NICO. Fudhopp. I wysyła córkę przez lasu z trzema rozkazami. (I visiwa tchurkan pshes lassu z chrema rozkazami.) [And he sends his daughter out across the forest with three rules.]

GRIGORI. And he send out daughter with three rule.

NICO. Pierwszy rozkaz; nie rozmawjaj z obcymi ludzmi. (Pyervishi rozkazi; nye rozmayvi z obtsimi ludjmi.) [One – talk to no stranger.]

GRIGORI. Talk to no stranger – one.

NICO. Drugi rozkaz: trzymaj się ścieżki   . Trzeci rozkaz: nie jeść jedzenia z lasu. (Drugi rozkaz: trzhimay shen shcheshki. Chrechi rozkaz: nye yesht yedzeniya z lassu.) [Two: keep to the path. Three: do not eat food of the forest.]

GRIGORI. Keep all of way to path, two, and three, she forbid from pick up food of forest.

NICO. Eat.

GRIGORI. Forbid from eating food of forest.

NICO. A po trzech godzinakh nie wróciła. (A po chrekh godjinakh nye vroochiwa.) [And three hours later she had not returned.

GRIGORI. And three hour later she not return.

NICO. I wysyła syna poszukać. (I visiwa siyna poshukach.) [And he sends the son to look.]

GRIGORI. And so father send off son to look for her.

NICO. I syn znajduję v lasu . . . (I siyn znayduyen v lassu . . .) [And the son finds in the forest . . .]

GRIGORI. And the son finds in the forest . . .

NICO (*graphically*). . . . . Kupę pociętych ramją i nóg i kawałki ciała – (Koopen pochentikh ramyan i nog i kavawki chowa –) [. . . a pile of bits of dismembered limbs and cut up arms and bits of body –]

GRIGORI. Hey actually you know I don't think this so good.

Very slight pause.

AMIRA. OK. I hear it differently. I hear it not ordinary woodchopper. But king. And not ordinary son, but hero.

MARINA (*Russian*). Shto praiskhodit? [What's happening?]

NICO (*Polish*). Królewcz wyjeżda w daleką podrósz. (Kroolevich viyezhdzha v dalekan podroozh.) [There is a king's son going on a journey.]

MARINA (*enthusiastically*). Ah. Tsaryevich.

AMIRA. Yes, good, he set out on a journey –

NICO. Wielka wyprawa . . . (Vyelka viprava . . .) [A great expedition . . .]

AMIRA. Or why not, yes, there set out hero with great army –

GRIGORI. Expedition . . .

NICO. . . . przez drogi mlecznę . . . (. . . pshes drogi mlechnen . . .)
[. . . through the galaxies . . .]

AMIRA. Which together journey through the . . .

NICO. . . . żeby przelecic przez ostateczną granicę . . . . (. . . rshebi
pshelechich pshez ostatechnan granitsen . . .) [. . . to cross the
final frontier . . .]

AMIRA. Crossing last border . . .

NICO. Smialę lecic tam gdzie nikogo jeszcze nie było, w – (Smayale
lechich tam gdzhe nikogo yeshche nye biwo v –) [. . . boldly
going where no man had gone before in –]

GRIGORI. I think he say –

NICO. – Starship Enterprise.

AMIRA (*dismissively*). It Starship. Dr Spock. Boldly going where no
man is gone before.

NICO. Space – the final frontier.

RAIF. Hey. Beam me up Scotty.

NICO. Da.

To ANTONIO:

Uhura.

ANTONIO. OK. No starship. But small village, central Africa. And it
is World War Two and an aircraft officer, let us say from England,
is shot down and parachutes down in the village. And he is
naturally captured by the tribesmen who have never seen a white
man and they prepare their grandest pot to cook him in. And as
spear is raised to slice him up, he say: now look here chaps if you
will save my life I will tell you all the story of my military exploits
donchaknow. And the villagers who hadn't understood said, oh are
you a warrior? And he said, yes, well, you might say so. And they
were warriors so they jumped up and down. And they asked, is
your side winning in the war? And he said, yes, I think we can say
more or less that all in all we're winning. And the Africans throw
up their spears in joy. And how many of the other side d'you kill?
And he answered, well now actually you come to mention it I have
personally done in thirty of the blighters wizard show. And the
savages jump up and down and throw their spears in huge delight.
Dear fellow, thirty done in single-handed, what a feast you must
have had! And the officer says: gentlemen, I am from Europe,
cradle of world civilisation. We don't eat people where I come
from. 'Oh', say the Africans in puzzlement. 'So why d'you kill
them?'

He turns to RAIF *and* ABDUL, *who has picked up the essence of
the story from the gestures.*

ABDUL. Hey not spear. Kalashinikov.

ANTONIO *wants to involve* RAIF *and* ABDUL *in the game. So he shouts to them*:

ANTONIO. Who dare win.

RAIF. Hasta La Vista, baby.

Running to kick an imaginary ball at RAIF *and* ANTONIO:

ANTONIO. Go – o – oal!

ABDUL *goes into what might be a kind of sword dance if he had a sword, with* RAIF *accompanying, beating out the rhythm on a petrol drum. Then* NICO *enters the circle with an impressive Romany dancing turn, involving first* MARINA, *then* AMIRA *and eventually* CLEOPATRA *in a swirling fandango. All the* REFUGEES *except* YASMIN, FATIMA *and* TUNU *become caught up in the dance. Then* TUNU *comes forward with her story.*

TUNU. OK. (*Sinhalese*). mama kathandarayak kiyannang. [I'll tell you a story.]

TUNU*'s story is initially incomprehensible as no-one but her speaks her language. But gradually, through a kind of collective reading of the story, supplemented by* TUNU*'s own hints, confirmations, corrections and echoes of the other* STORYTELLERS' *gestural language – for 'king', 'expedition', 'capture', going into a forest, giving a gift and so on – the story emerges and becomes clear.*

TUNU. Ékamath éka rataka, hitiya Dhasharartha kiyala hungak balasampanne rajathunék. [Once upon a time there lived a very powerful king called Dhasharartha.]

GRIGORI. King.

TUNU. Unwahanséta hitiya bisawak, mé bisawa hungak papuru, ahankara ganiyek. [His highness had a wife, who was a cruel and conceited woman.]

MARINA. Tsarevna.

AMIRA (*Russian*). Zhestokaya. [Malicious.]

TUNU. Unwahanséta thawath hitiya puthék. Puthagé name Rama. Ishwara déviyangé dunne bindala Rama, Sita dinagaththa. Mé atharathuré Dhasharartha rajathuma thamangé rajakama Rama kumarayate pavaranne kalpana kéruwa. [He also had a son, and the son's name was Rama. Prince Rama proved his great strength by snapping Lord Ishawara's bow in two and won the beautiful Princess Sita. In the meantime, King Dhasharartha decided to hand over his kingdom to Rama.]

MARINA (*to* GRIGORI). Atkazatsa ot prestola? [Abdicate?]

TUNU. Namuth unwahanségé napuru bisawate mégana irisiya hithila Rama kumarayawe awrudu dhahahatharakate vanantharayate pituwahal kérewwa. [But in jealousy his cruel queen had Rama banished to the woods for fourteen years.]

GRIGORI. Execution?

YASMIN. Exile.

TUNU. Ithin, Rama Sita kumariya samaga vanagatha vuna. Vanantharayé dakke thapasayék Rama kumarayate vidya balaya athi eethalayak dunna. [So Rama sets off into the woods with Sita. A hermit they meet in the forest gives Rama a magic arrow.]

YASMIN (to CLEOPATRA). Holy man.

TUNU. Mé atharathure Ravana – [In the meantime Ravana –]

GRIGORI. This Rama still?

TUNU. Ravana.

GRIGORI. Sorry.

TUNU. Ravana kiyana rakus raja Sita kumariya dake, Sitawe labaganne kalpanakéruwa. Ithin Rama gethara hitiya nathi velawake, Ravana balahathkarayén Sita kumariyawe thamangé dupathate paharegenagiya. Ithin Rama visala hamudavak raskaragéna thamangé raté indala Ravana rajugé dupathate palamák hadanne theeranaya kela. [Ravana the Demon king claps eyes on Sita and decides he must have her. So at a moment when Rama is not about, Ravanna abducts Sita and carries her across the seas to his island. So Rama gathers himself an enormous army and starts building a bridge from his homeland to Ravana's island.]

AMIRA. He – make boat? Build bridge? to Sita.

TUNU. Visala yuddhayakate pasuwe Rama saha Ravana moonate moona hambawuna. Namuth éka oluwak angin wénwénakota thavath oluwak Ravana rajugé kandin mathuwénawa. Anthimata, Rama éyayge vidya balaya athi eethalaya aragéna Ravana rajuwe marumuwate pathkela. Yuddayen pasuwa Rama saha Sita navatha ekathuvuna. [After a terrible and bloody battle, Rama and Ravana finally engage in mortal combat. But, to his dismay, Rama finds that every time he manages to lop one of Ravana's many heads off another grows in its place. But then Rama remembers his magic arrow – and shoots Ravana dead. And after the battle Rama and Sita are reunited.]

MOST PEOPLE respond as if this was the end; a smattering of applause.

TUNU. Namuth, Rama, Sita ayagé pathivatha rekagéna hitiyé nè kiyala sèka pahalakéruwa. [But Rama doubts Sita's faith.]

The LISTENERS look blank, and whisper questions to each other.

MARINA (Russian). Shto ana gavarit? [What is she saying?]

GRIGORI (Russian). Ya nye znayoo. [I don't know.]

TUNU. Sita mégana dukwéla, visala ginimaleyak gahala ginnata pènna. Namuth aya pichchune nè. Mokadha, aya thamungé pathivatha rèkagéna hitapu nisa. [Sita, hugely saddened by his distrust of her, makes herself a pyre and throws herself upon it. But because she has been faithful she doesn't burn.]

AMIRA. I think – Rama doubt if Sita faithful during her captivity.

TUNU *nods.*

AMIRA. And so to prove she build great fire and throw herself within. But she suffers no harm.

TUNU *nods.*

TUNU. Ithin anthimata, Rama saha Sita, thamangé ratate gos hondin rajakamkela. [And so in the end Rama and Sita return to claim their kingdom and live happily for all eternity.]

YASMIN (*trying to be harsher than she feels*). Oh yes, of course. And they live happily for ever afterwards.

OLIVER, *caught up in the story, whispers to* GABRIELLA.

OLIVER. Or as we might more readily remember it: a God forbids his child the forest fruit . . .

OLIVER *realises he is being heard by the* HOSTAGE-TAKERS. *He decides to tell his story; perhaps he too echoing the gestures of proscription, banishment, capture and death:*

OLIVER. Or as we might remember it: a God forbids his child the forest fruit. The child of disobedience is banished and his children are condemned to wander through the earth. But finally the God in pity sends his only son for their redemption. Who teaches them through parables and tales. Who rides unrecognised into the holy city. Prophesies his capture and his death. But promises his followers that nonetheless, in three days' time he'll prove himself the thing he claims to be.

Slight pause. AMIRA *steps towards* OLIVER.

AMIRA. And then? And then?

OLIVER *is being invited into the circle to finish his story. Suddenly,* FATIMA *bursts into the circle. She is furious.*

FATIMA (*Turkish*). Ama bu, bu olmamalı. Biz bu insanlarla oturup masal anlatıyoruz. Onlar emperyalistler ishkenjejiler. Onlar bizim eseerlerimiz, onlara göz kulak olmalıyız. Onlar öldürmekle tehdeed ettik. Shimdi onları nasıl öldürürüz sonra? Bizim hakkımızda ne düshünejekler? [This is – this must not happen. We are sitting here telling infant's stories, with these people. They are imperialists and torturers. They are our captives and we must keep them secure. We have threatened to kill them. How can we kill them now? What will they think of us?]

Slight pause.

Elleri, ayakları baalanmalı ve aaızları tıkanmalı! Onlarla hich konushmamalıyız! [They must be bound and gagged! We mustn't speak to them!]

She storms off to the side. AMIRA *feels she must explain* FATIMA*'s outburst to the* HOSTAGES.

AMIRA. She was with the PKK. They are kind of army, fighting for Kurdistan. Her brother turn up, he is driven crazy. She take him home to where her mother keep her son. She is deserter. They kill her if they catch her. And there she find . . .

OLIVER. Yes. Yes, I know.

Slight pause.

I wonder. How you grieve. When you find that. How you lament.

The baby begins to cry. CLEOPATRA *and* TUNU *go to fetch the baby. She is brought in, and comforted. The baby becomes a focus:* PEOPLE *group round. The beginnings of a lullaby.* YASMIN *jangles her keys at the baby.* YASMIN *catches* AMIRA*'s eye.*

YASMIN. It is – my house keys. From Kuwait City. It is crazy that I keep them.

Slight pause.

It is like your photos I suppose.

AMIRA *goes to the* HOSTAGES.

AMIRA. OK. It is like this. I have a cousin. Who is Muslim sure but sophisticated European woman. She is taken from her house by lorry to an iron ore plant. Then they transfer her to what had been a tile factory. Then the men are separated out and they go 'shopping'. While the women are transported to an elementary school. For what is called 'exchange'.

Gesturing to FATIMA.

She is Muslim. In Koran, it say: 'Whoever is removed from fire and admitted unto paradise, shall win great victory'. 'The present life is but delusion'. 'We all belong to God and to Him we shall return'.

OLIVER. What does that mean?

AMIRA. It means that only Muslim true believer of the resurrection. It is for them great blasphemy, to despair at a loved one being called to God.

LEO. For 'them'? Is all of this about a 'them'. Or you?

AMIRA *can't answer. She goes to sit with her cello.*

YASMIN. So. Not so much a fairy tale.

Slight pause. She approaches the HOSTAGES, *pointing at* FATIMA.

When she came back at first it looked quite normal. And as it was the morning it was no surprise to find the door was open, and the door down to the cellar also. The neighbours came and shouted at her not to go. Down the steps the first thing that she notices was the care with which the sheet was laid out on the ground. Just the faintest outline of a child's shape. As if maybe he was asleep beneath it. Or even for a moment that he wasn't there.

Suddenly, the deep, long, sad tone of a cello. AMIRA has started to play. Singing begins, over the cello. It's a kind of lament. It swells and fades. And then, as the first shafts of light appear through the high windows and across the painting, there is a sudden heavy drumming on the door.

Scene Seven

It is dawn. Shafts of light through the high windows catch the painting: the star in the sky and St John's arm stretched out towards the Virgin; we can just see the rock in the foreground. EVERYONE stands still, silenced by the knocking. YASMIN, who is nearest, shins up the ladder. She looks out, and turns. To RAIF:

YASMIN (*Arabic*). iftaH al-baab. [Open the door.]

As YASMIN descends, RAIF and ABDUL open the door. Father KAROLYI enters, naked, holding up a piece of paper. He walks into the centre of the nave. No-one moves.

KAROLYI. You said. I understood. You would admit only a naked priest. I am Father Petr Karolyi.

With the paper:

I have the answer to your demands.

Pause.

Can I please have – something to cover me?

AMIRA finds him a coat. KAROLYI puts the paper in his teeth and puts on the coat. Then he takes the paper from his mouth.

AMIRA. Is this your church, Father?

KAROLYI. It is your church. As is surely clear to everyone.

YASMIN. So we will have our answer please. Or do you want us to fulfil our promise?

KAROLYI. Promise?

YASMIN. Threat.

Slight pause.

KAROLYI. I am so sorry. Yes, of course.

Addressing the paper:

First of all, of course, the national authorities must make clear that in considering your requests –

RAIF. Demands!

KAROLYI. – they cannot accede to threats of violence.

YASMIN *gestures dismissively.*

KAROLYI. On the other hand, as a gesture of humanitarianism, your 'demands' have been passed on to the internal ministries of concerned countries. And have been considered. In as – generous a light as possible. In accordance naturally with United Nations Convention on Refugees of 1951 . . .

He senses impatience.

Etcetera. So, first of all. And on condition as you must expect that all the hostages are released unharmed . . . the following is the result.

He goes through the list:

The woman T, of Sri Lankan origin. A religious charity in Savonlinna, Finland, has agreed to sponsor. So she is admitted there. RH – Azerbaijan – is deemed to be at risk of persecution living in territory presently Armenian. So he is OK for Germany. The Bosnian family N, C and baby P are granted emergency asylum on the grounds of the baby and their residence in Bosnia.

GRIGORI *snorts.*

MNN, originally of Latvia, has been subject to political discrimination – persecution – and has been invited by an American foundation to make a new life in Pittsburg, Pennsylvania. And finally YA, former Kuwait resident, is stateless clearly. And is offered refuge under regulation for emergency humanitarian admission in Holland, Canada or Denmark. So, some choice there.

He has finished, and folds the paper.

YASMIN. That's it?

KAROLYI. That's it.

GRIGORI. And what about about the rest of us?

KAROLYI. I must guess your applications – your demands – were unsuccessful.

GRIGORI. This fantasy. These not Bosnian. They Polish, if anything at all.

KAROLYI. I'm so sorry.

GRIGORI. Look, I explain. I am ethnic German. I say in application. I explain.

KAROLYI. I am just a messenger.

YASMIN (*to* ANTONIO). This is transparent.

ANTONIO. But you are OK.

ABDUL (*Turkish*). Meni sokhajakhlar? [Well? Am I to be admitted?]

RAIF (*to* ADBUL, *in Azeri*). Chokh üzüldüm, meni sokhtular, seni degil. [I am so sorry. They let me in, but not you.]

ABDUL (*Turkish*). Ne? [What?]

GRIGORI. You let in gypsies, but not hard worker.

ABDUL (*Turkish, to* RAIF). Roosee oldugun ichin sokhtular seni. [They let you in, because you are Russian!]

RAIF (*Azeri*). Men Roosee deyilim. [I am not Russian.]

GRIGORI. You admit Muslims but not Christian people.

KAROLYI. 'I' am doing nothing.

GRIGORI. You admit this woman who lives forty years in Latvia –

MARINA (*Russian*). Shto on gavareet? [What is he saying?]

GRIGORI. – and in all that time does not learn word for bread.

MARINA (*Russian*). Minya razreshen v'yezd? [Have I been admitted?]

KAROLYI. I am most sorry, but –

GRIGORI. You let in Muslim, let in gypsy –

LEO. What is the situation with the Kurd?

Slight pause.

MARINA (*Russian, to* ANTONIO). Pazhalsta, minya poostili? [Please, am I admitted?]

LEO. Please.

ANTONIO (*Russian, bleakly*). Da, poostili. Pazdravlyayoo. [Yes, you are admitted. Congratulations.]

LEO. What please is the position of this woman here?

Pause.

KAROLYI. I'm sorry?

LEO *points to* FATIMA, *who is still with* GABRIELLA. *Pause.*

LEO. By what conceivable criteria of selection. Can this woman be excluded from the list of people threatened by political and religious persecution?

KAROLYI. Oh, Professor Katz. In this part of Europe, it is a little arbitrary sometimes, whether one is cast as victim or accomplice. An invader or a liberator. The object of unjust persecution or a voluntary exile.

GRIGORI. And so what happens to the rest of us? Those not 'selected'?

KAROLYI. There is a bus in half an hour.

AMIRA. To take us where?

KAROLYI. Well, naturally, the border.

ANTONIO. Which? Which border?

KAROLYI. The one you crossed two days ago. As you must surely have expected.

ABDUL (*Turkish*). Ne diyor? [What does he say?] (*Russian.*) Shto on gavarit? [What does he say?]

RAIF. Shto praiskhodit? [What's going on?]

FATIMA (*Turkish*). Ne oluyor? Ne diyorlar? [What's happening? What are they saying?]

ABDUL (*Turkish*). Bizi laade etmekh istiyorlar gaaliba. [They want to send us back.]

MARINA (*Russian*). Shto praiskhodit? [What is going on?]

ANTONIO (*Russian*). On gavarit shto nas viyshloot abratna. [He says that we will be deported back.]

KAROLYI. It is as you must acknowledge generous. There are no arrests, no charges. If you go.

AMIRA *stands, buttons her coat, picks up her cello and walks to the door. She sits.* KAROLYI *looks at his list.*

AMIRA. AR. From Sarajevo. But now not so chic.

KAROLYI. So now everybody must I think decide.

ANTONIO *assembles* ABDUL *and* GRIGORI *to confer.*

ANTONIO (*Russian*). Nam biy nado ab ctom pagavarit. [Now we must talk about this.]

GRIGORI (*Russian*). Eta zhe prosta byezooiye. [This is crazy.]

YASMIN *wants to join but is excluded.* RAIF *is clearly unwelcome too. In the background,* FATIMA *and* ABDUL *confer.*

LEO. So what's the game?

KAROLYI. There is no game.

OLIVER. And all of this is true?

The phone rings. YASMIN *beats* ANTONIO *to answer it.*

YASMIN. Hallo? Hallo.

Slight pause.

No it is not. Do you speak English?

ANTONIO *has his hand out for the phone.* YASMIN, *impatient*:
Hold on. Hold on.

She has no choice but to hand the phone to ANTONIO. *To cover:*

It seems the English-speaking man is only days.

ANTONIO (*Russian*). Viy pa-rooski gavaritye? [Do you speak Russian?]

Slight pause.

Da, on zdyes, ya payidoo za nim. [Yes, he is here. I'll get him for you.]

To KAROLYI:

It's for you.

KAROLYI *comes to the phone. As he takes it,* ANTONIO *looks coldly at* YASMIN.

KAROLYI (*down the phone, speaking in the language of our country*). Obazhda se Karolyi. Obsuzhdat predlozhenieto. [It's Karolyi. They are considering the offer.]

LEO. What's he saying?

GABRIELLA (*shrugs*). That they considering.

KAROLYI. Da, da. Kakvo? Kolko? [Yes, yes. What? How many?]

Slight pause.

Da, shte im kazha. Da. [Yes, I'll tell them. Yes.].

Still holding the phone, he turns to YASMIN.

YASMIN. Well?

KAROLYI. I'm afraid there is a complication.

YASMIN. Oh, I see.

KAROLYI. It is not in my hands. Nor those of the authorities.

YASMIN. No, no. Of course not.

ANTONIO. Please, go on.

KAROLYI. It is that apparently a crowd – well, more a mob, is forming –

GRIGORI. A mob?

KAROLYI. – of people, you know, close-cropped – skinheads. And they are demanding that the police will storm the building. Or else they threaten they'll do it themselves.

He hears words from the phone and lifts it to his ear. He listens, then, in our country's language:

Razbira se. [Of course.]

To YASMIN:

And the police are fearful that unless we can evacuate the building soon –

ANTONIO. How many people?

KAROLYI. They say at least a hundred.

YASMIN. Armed?

KAROLYI (*down phone*). Pitat dali sa vu'oruzheni. [They are asking, are they armed?]

Slight pause.

Giob'yo? Kakvi giob'yo? [Rocks? What sort of rocks?]

To the REFUGEES:

As yet they do not seem, the people who are there, to have firearms. Yet. Just sticks and rocks. So the police will bring the bus up to the church in a quarter of an hour.

OLIVER. Did you say 'rocks'?

KAROLYI. Yes, only rocks. So far.

Now TUNU *gathers her possessions and moves to the exit, followed by* MARINA. GRIGORI *looks fearfully to* ANTONIO.

YASMIN. Give me that phone.

She snatches the telephone from KAROLYI. *Down phone:*

Now we know why fascists were so welcome in your country!

She slams the phone down.

KAROLYI. That will not I think be very helpful.

RAIF (*Azeri*). Ne yapıyorsun? [What are you doing?] (*English.*) What this you do?

YASMIN. Oh, come on. Do you believe this for a moment? They will take you into Germany? This is all bullshit.

KAROLYI. This is not bullshit.

OLIVER. Um, excuse me –

YASMIN. OK, now. No more shit. We demand – now – we are taken, in a bloc . . .

OLIVER. Excuse me . . .

NICO *picks up his release is threatened.*

YASMIN. . . . . in a single bloc . . . .

OLIVER. Excuse me, what word did you use?

YASMIN. . . . . to and *across* the German border . . .

KAROLYI. I'm afraid that I say 'bullshit'.

YASMIN. . . . . . where we are given all EC work permits . . .

OLIVER. No, I meant, before.

KAROLYI (*to* YASMIN). Now, please, you surely understand –

YASMIN. And we will take – two hostages with us. As *you* will surely understand.

OLIVER. The word for rock.

YASMIN. And unless we have transport for that purpose here in a quarter of an hour . . .

YASMIN goes and picks up one of the petrol cans.

OLIVER (*to* GABRIELLA). The word he used for rock.

GABRIELLA (*offhand*). He say 'giob'yo'. It is old word.

YASMIN. . . . then we fulfil our threat.

She gestures to ABDUL to get the other can as she climbs on to the platform.

OLIVER. Old word?

GABRIELLA. Old language word. I tell you. Oliver –

YASMIN. And in Professor Katz's telling phrase we fry this greatest artfind of the century right off the wall.

From the platform; defiantly, to KAROLYI:

OK? You understand me now?

KAROLYI. But, I'm afraid that this is not correct.

Slight pause.

YASMIN. You do, you read our statement?

KAROLYI. Yes, of course. But I'm afraid that you are misinformed. The painting is of very little value.

Slight pause.

YASMIN. Sorry?

KAROLYI. It was thought at one time that it was painted in the early thirteenth century and thus of great value as you say. But despite all efforts by these most distinguished art historians, it has not been proved. It is a matter of regret to many of us. But the painting has no real worth. To this place, this country. Or to you. So now, maybe, you are ready for the bus?

Pause. YASMIN *turns to* LEO.

YASMIN. Oh, oh. Professor Katz.

GABRIELLA. Please, Father –

YASMIN. Lies. And more lies.

To RAIF *and* ANTONIO, *as she descends the ladder.*

Hold him!

LEO. Hey –

YASMIN. We can believe no-one.

To GRIGORI:

YASMIN. You want to get to Germany? You hold him.

GRIGORI *takes* LEO.

LEO. Hey, what is this.

YASMIN. And then I think at least we are believed. That having killed one, we will kill another.

LEO. Jesus Christ –

YASMIN (*to* ANTONIO). Give me the pistol.

KAROLYI. Please, no, this is madness.

RAIF (*with a step towards* YASMIN, *in Azeri*). Sus, heyejanlanma . . . [Quiet, don't get excited . . .]

YASMIN. Antonio. give me the gun. Give it to me.

OLIVER *steps between* ANTONIO *and* YASMIN.

OLIVER. No, don't.

YASMIN. Oh, come now, please. The gun.

OLIVER. For one – because, he's right. It's madness. If anyone is killed. You'll none of you get anywhere.

ANTONIO *is not moving.*

For two, yes, sure, he lied. But wouldn't you?

KAROLYI. Dr Davenport –

OLIVER. For three – because – it could be – he was right.

ANTONIO. What's right?

OLIVER. The painting. It is – it may well be – your lifeline after all.

YASMIN. Oh yes? And why is this?

OLIVER. Because the word for rock in the old language of this country, is 'gobbyo'. As 'lora' is the word for star.

ABDUL (*Arabic*). eysh yagool. [What is he saying?]

YASMIN (*Arabic*). yabdoo innoo injann iz-zalami. [I think he's gone berserk.]

OLIVER. Which if you give me just three minutes, I'll explain.

Pause. ANTONIO *lowers his gun.* YASMIN *shrugs.* OLIVER *points up at the painting.*

OLIVER. For where this painting has ten stars, or 'lora', Giotto's has ten wildly grieving angels. And where this has a boulder, Giotto has a second woman painted from behind. In a kind of huddled, sort of, humpy shouldered pose. And 'gobbo' is, in fact. Is as it happens. The Italian for 'hunchback'. As 'dolore' is for 'grief'.

Pause. GRIGORI *leaves* LEO. ABDUL *too moves a little apart.*

And of course this could be easily explained by someone misdescribing Giotto's fresco to a painter here . . . But for the fact that by the time that Giotto painted what he painted, describing anything in your old language was to put it mildly ill-advised.

Slight pause.

ANTONIO. Now this most interesting –

YASMIN (*looks at her watch*). This is shit –

OLIVER. No. This is proof that we were right.

He is on the ladder up to the painting.

You see, the problem is. We have this mindset, still, about the mediaeval period. That everybody knows their places, no-one travels, no-one moves. To each his own walled garden. Whereas actually mediaeval Europe was a chaos of diaspora. Every frontier teeming, every crossroads thronged. So it is frankly more than possible that a painter could have set off in the early years of the thirteenth century. From what perils we cannot imagine. And coming to this place, and being taken captive, and offering for his release to paint a picture, here, so akin to nature that its figures seem to live and breathe . . .

AMIRA *stands and moves closer to look at the painting.*

And employing for that purpose a particularly vital but as yet unknown deep blue. For the simple reason – that he brought it with him.

LEO. Sorry?

GABRIELLA. Like taxis.

LEO. Taxis?

OLIVER. Yes. Not going to the east, but coming from. Boldly going where no painter went before.

GABRIELLA *doesn't understand.*

GABRIELLA. What you mean, he is – Italian explorer?

OLIVER. No I mean, I think he was an Arab.

Pause.

LEO (*delicately*). An Arab Figurative Painter? Early thirteenth century?

Now OLIVER *is on the platform in front of the painting.*

OLIVER. Yes. Absolutely and precisely so. An Arab colourist, who learns his fresco in the monasteries of Serbia or Macedonia. Who sees the great mosaics of the mighty churches of Constantinople.

And who thinks, like any artist, I could do that too. And having
thought some more, that he could do it better. But his huge
advantage over almost everybody else is not just that he has the
classic geometry the Arabs kept alive for the best part of 800 years,
nor yet again the optics they hypothesised around the first
millennium, but the fact that nobody's explained to him that
painters aren't supposed to use them. So he has two eyes, and they
tell him things have three dimensions, and he paints the world that
way. With all that innocence, that freshness and that rage, we bring
to things when we come up against them for the very first – first
time.

GABRIELLA *moves near the bottom of the ladder.*

GABRIELLA. Because, for him – it is.

OLIVER. Exactly.

GABRIELLA. And so they tell him this strange story.

OLIVER. Of a woman who has see her son die on a tree.

LEO. Shortly after he had told her and his followers –

GABRIELLA. That he will die –

OLIVER. But rise again in three days' time.

LEO. So for him the story's not about her weight of grief –

GABRIELLA. But actually –

OLIVER. – her want of faith.

He's at St John.

He's not reaching out to comfort her at all. He's reaching out to
warn her. It's an act of admonition.

To AMIRA:

Because he know, and like the man who painted him, believed, if
you are taken from the fire, you gain a mighty victory.

LEO. Our present life is but delusion.

GABRIELLA. That we all belong to God and to Him we shall return.

OLIVER. And should you not believe that even more, if your son has
promised you there is eternal life, and in three days' time he'll rise
again, and prove it?

Pause. It sinks in.

GABRIELLA. So then it true.

OLIVER. It's true.

GABRIELLA. Well – tallyho.

Pause. AMIRA *is looking up in wonder at the painting.*

AMIRA. Well. Glory be.

OLIVER. Well glory be indeed.

Pause.

YASMIN. So, then. We need not kill Professor Katz to show that we mean business.

LEO *looks bleakly at* YASMIN.

LEO. Well. Good.

YASMIN. We need only to destroy this painting.

YASMIN *pushes past* GABRIELLA *and climbs up the ladder.*

GABRIELLA. No.

YASMIN (*calling behind her, in Arabic*). haat al-banzeen. [Bring the petrol.]

Turning to see no-one move:

That is, if anybody wishes to get out of here.

ABDUL, *shrugging, picks up the second petrol can.*

OLIVER. Now surely, you can't think of –

YASMIN. Try me.

GABRIELLA. But don't you see – it is your painting.

The telephone rings. ABDUL *to the ladder.*

YASMIN. Aha. The telephone.

KAROLYI *goes to the telephone.* ABDUL *is nearly at the platform with his can.*

YASMIN (*to* KAROLYI). You can tell them what is happening.

AMIRA (*Russian, to* ANTONIO). Eto prosta byezoomiye. Da astanavi zhe yeyo. [This is insane, please stop her.]

YASMIN. Secure the hostages!

KAROLYI (*down phone*). Allo? Karolyi.

ABDUL (*shouts behind him, to* RAIF, *in Turkish*). Rehinlere göz qulaq ol, onları qachırmayın! [Keep an eye on the hostages, don't let them escape!] Grigori!

ABDUL *hands* GRIGORI *the gun.* RAIF *and* ANTONIO, *a little uncertainly, move in on* LEO *and* GABRIELLA.

LEO. Now this is *really* crazy.

KAROLYI (*our country*); Kato che li igrata zagroobyava. [Things are getting ugly.]

YASMIN (*to* ABDUL, *Arabic*). khalleek jaahiz inta wal-banzeen. [OK, be sure the petrol's ready.]

She hurries down the ladder as ABDUL *prepares to douse the painting with petrol.* GRIGORI *has a weapon.* RAIF *shouts at* MARINA:

RAIF (*Russian*). Von at dvyeri! Von at dvyeri! [Get away from the door!]

GABRIELLA. Don't let this happen.

OLIVER (*to* ABDUL). Please. Please, I beg you –

KAROLYI (*our country*). Da mislya che sega. [Yes I think now.]

AMIRA (*to* ANTONIO *in Russian*). Astanavi eto, prashoo vas! [Stop this! Please!]

YASMIN (*to* KAROYLI). OK. Now, tell them. That they have exactly five –

   ABDUL *is about to douse the painting. There is a sudden explosion. It is not immediately clear where from. Engines rev, sirens wail. Smoke billows. Armed* COMMANDOES *in black uniforms and balaclavas burst through a gaping hole that has appeared in the painting, on to the platform. They see* OLIVER *there.*

FIRST COMMANDO. Terrorist? Terrorist?

OLIVER. Uh –

   OLIVER *of course looks like a refugee. The* COMMANDO *shoots him dead. Neither* ANTONIO, GRIGORI *nor* RAIF *can fire.* YASMIN *grabs* GRIGORI's *weapon.*

YASMIN (*Arabic*). aacteeni iyyaah. [Give that to me.]

   The FIRST COMMANDO *shoots* YASMIN *dead.* ABDUL *dives to the deck.* RAIF *raises his weapon and the* SECOND COMMANDO *shoots him dead.* ANTONIO *drops his weapon, but he is shot by the* SECOND COMMANDO. TUNU *makes a run for it, but the* FIRST COMMANDO *shoots her. The* SECOND COMMANDO *has* LEO *and* GABRIELLA *on the floor.*

SECOND COMMANDO. Tu est terroriste? Tu est terroriste?

LEO. No I'm not a fucking terrorist. I'm a fucking art historian.

   CLEOPATRA *grabs her pram and makes a dash for the door.*

CLEOPATRA. My infant. Infant, infant, infant! Tallyho!

   CLEOPATRA *makes it through the door.*

SECOND COMMANDO (*to* GABRIELLA). You terrorist?

LEO. And so is she.

FIRST COMMANDO. Jemand getroffen? [Has anybody scored?]

SECOND COMMANDO (*shouts back*). Zwei hier! [Two here!]

FIRST COMMANDO (*shouts*). Nieder halten. Alle fichen nieder! [Everyone down. Everyone fucking keep down!] (*English.*) Keep fucking down!

   The smoke is clearing; the sirens and the engines beginning to die.

Scene Eight

*A few hours later. On the floor are red plastic flags with attached
labels, marking where the dead REFUGEES (and OLIVER) lay. LEO
stands with Mikhail CZABA and Anna JEDLIKOVA. LEO has
returned from debriefing ostensibly to fetch his files. He holds
AMIRA's broken cello in his hands. He's very angry.*

LEO. So you were there throughout?

CZABA. You bet. I am Minister for Preservation of our National
   Monuments. And Mrs Jedlikova is observer from our Ministry of
   Law and Order.

LEO (*looking round, bitterly*). Preservation.

JEDLIKOVA. Certainly of law.

   LEO looks at the little red flags.

CZABA. It most sophisticated. First you limit access of world outside.
   Move everything from field of vision. Don't give phone number so
   they must always wait for you to call. Change over guy on phone
   so different languages. Then slowly build up their routine. You
   order mealtime. Control all aspect of environment. Heat, light. And
   gradually they are turn to child.

LEO. I'm sorry?

CZABA. All part of softly softly catch your monkey.

LEO (*waving round at the scene*). Though not – in this case – with
   demonstrable success.

   Pause.

CZABA. Well, no. Agreed.

   Slight pause.

   In fact, there big dispute. Between all European counter-terrorist,
   who say, negotiate, you get through first two days, out of long
   grass. But also wiseguys from America, who say, if you don't clean
   up in two day, you send in US cavalry. So they prepare two
   gameplan. One if Karolyi will succeed. And one if plan go belly
   up. And unfortunately belly up she go. And so – bouf – Pax
   Vespucciana.

   LEO looks to CZABA.

JEDLIKOVA. I think it not so much 'unfortunate'. I think there is big
   risk hostages are killed.

CZABA. Beg pardon. Your friend's joke I think.

LEO. So then you heard it all.

   Pause.

CZABA. Of course.

LEO. They bust the bug.

CZABA. Ah, wonders of your English language.

LEO. *What*?

CZABA. They bust *a* bug. *The* bug was in *the* syringe.

LEO. And presumably, they were supposed to?

CZABA (*smiling*). Sure. Presumably.

LEO. And you hear everything?

CZABA (*smiling*). Hey. Talk of fucking Tower of Babel.

CZABA *realises* LEO *is concerned.*

Hey, listen up. They say, you will be bound to bond. In fact, it whole idea. No-one hold one word you say against you.

GABRIELLA *stands in doorway. She has a borrrowed overcoat and* CLEOPATRA*'s pram.*

GABRIELLA. Well, that I must say great relief.

LEO, CZABA *and* JEDLIKOVA *look over to* GABRIELLA *who gently pushes the pram over towards them. We see that a swastika has been spray-painted on the side.* EVERYONE *takes this in. Then*:

GABRIELLA. Voilà.

Slight pause. CZABA *to* LEO:

CZABA. Look. We are young poor country. Our industry is junkyard and our currency confetti. So, no, we cannot be dumping ground for everybody's rejects.

To GABRIELLA:

Of course I so choked about your friend. And this. And that. But still. So sorry. No.

He goes out. Pause.

LEO. Uh, d'you know, if she, if they . . .

GABRIELLA. Have no idea.

Slight pause.

Well, if she survive. Maybe her father will not sell her baby now.

JEDLIKOVA. Yes. Yes, we hear this. Terrible.

GABRIELLA. You hear?

LEO. They heard it all.

Slight pause.

GABRIELLA. So they know that painting real.

JEDLIKOVA. I think – by this time – no-one very much is listening.

LEO. Yuh, sure. Shoot first, ask questions later. Ausländer verboten. Welcome to the West.

Pause. JEDLIKOVA *feels she must respond.*

JEDLIKOVA. Look. I know how it appear. What happen in this country since great turnaround.

Slight pause.

But you must understand what we are losing during all this century. How communism strip away all culture from our past, and clothe us all instead in uniform. And when we throw it off we think, hey, we have been through all so much, we are new kind of people, we will build new life.

Slight pause.

But we find that we are not so special. Even those of us who suffer very much. And so yes, we turn from proletcult to Rambo, or pornography. And you know, is maybe best we march to next millennium in silly national costume. When alternative is dress of Arnold Schwarzenegger, or wearing nothing very much at all.

Slight pause.

It is, apparently, the weakest wall.

She goes out. LEO *and* GABRIELLA *are left together.*

GABRIELLA. Well. Church. Mosque. Stable. Torture centre. Foodstore. Fortress. Cemetery.

Slight pause.

Middle Europe theme park? Sure.

LEO. Hey. Gab. I am – so sorry.

Slight pause. GABRIELLA *takes* CLEOPATRA's *notebook from the pram. She opens it and reads.*

GABRIELLA (*reads*). Roadblock. Closed-circuit. Permit.

LEO. But hey. Hey.

GABRIELLA. Shrapnel. Tarpaulin. Yes?

LEO. You must hang on to one thing.

GABRIELLA. Checkpoint. What?

LEO. That he was right.

Pause. GABRIELLA *looks up to* LEO.

That basically, we are the sum of all the people who've invaded us. We are, involuntarily, each other's guests.

Pause.

GABRIELLA. Transfer. Exchanges. School.

LEO *takes the book.*

LEO. Mercy mission.

Pause.

GABRIELLA. Ambush.

LEO. Convoy. Baggage handler.

GABRIELLA. Backlog.

LEO. Buffer. Buffet.

GABRIELLA. Quota.

LEO. Flight.

   Slight pause.

   Chevrolet. Milkshake.

   Slight pause.

   Diaper. Princess.

   GABRIELLA *isn't going. He turns the pages.*

   Huddled.

GABRIELLA. Yearning?

LEO. Free.

   And the lights slowly fade.

   End of play.

And when the day of Pentecost was fully come, they were all with one accord in one place.

And suddenly there came a sound from heaven as of a rushing mighty wind, and it filled all the house where they were sitting. And there appeared unto them cloven tongues like as of fire, and it sat upon each of them. And they were all filled with the Holy Ghost, and began to speak with other tongues, as the Spirit gave them utterance . . .

And they were all amazed, and were in doubt, saying one to another, What meaneth this? Others mocking said, These men are full of new wine.

But Peter, standing up with the eleven, lifted up his voice, and said unto them, Ye Men of Judea, and all ye that dwell at Jerusalem, be this known unto you, and hearken to my words . . .

And it shall come to pass in the last days, saith God, I will pour out of my Spirit upon all flesh: and your sons and your daughters shall prophesy, and your young men shall see visions, and you old men shall dream dreams . . .

And all that believed were together, and had all things common; and sold their possessions and goods, and parted them to all men, as every man had need.

Acts of the Apostles, Chapter Two

A Nick Hern Book

This special programme edition of *Pentecost* first published
in Great Britain in 1995 by Nick Hern Books Limited,
14 Larden Road, London W3 7ST in association with the Royal
Shakespeare Company, Barbican Centre, London EC2Y 8BQ

Pentecost copyright © 1995 David Edgar

Typeset by Country Setting, Woodchurch, Kent TN26 3TB
Printed in Great Britain by Cox and Wyman Ltd, Reading, Berks

Reprinted 1998, 1999, 2000

A CIP catalogue record for this book is available from
the British Library

ISBN 1-85459-292 0

The front cover shows a detail of the fresco by Giotto di Bondone
called '*The Lamentation*' from the Cappella dei Scrovegni in Padua.

The inside front cover shows a sketch of the fresco 'discovered'
during the course of *Pentecost*.

The inside back cover shows a sketch of the complete '*Lamentation*'
by Giotto mentioned above.

Both sketches are by Robert Jones and are protected by copyright.